FISHING
the
LONG ISLAND COAST

FISHING
the
LONG ISLAND
COAST

TOM MELTON

BURFORD BOOKS

Copyright © 2005 by Tom Melton

All Rights Reserved. No part of this book may be reproduced in any manner without the express written consent of the publisher, except in cases of brief excerpts in critical reviews and articles. All inquiries should be addressed to: Burford Books, Inc., PO Box 388, Short Hills, NJ 07078.

10 9 8 7 6 5 4 3 2 1

Library of Congress Cataloging-in-Publication Data
　Melton, Tom.
　Fishing the Long Island coast / Tom Melton.
　　　p.　　cm.
　Includes index.
　ISBN 978-1-58080-129-4
　1. Saltwater fishing—New York (State)—Long Island—Guidebooks. 2. Fishing—New York (State)—Long Island—Guidebooks. 3. Long Island (N.Y.)—Guidebooks. I. Title.

SH529.M44　2005
799.16'09163'46—dc22

2005014614

CONTENTS

Dedication 7

Acknowledgments 8

Chapter 1. The Fish and How to Catch Them 9
Saltwater Species
Atlantic Cod • Blackfish • Black Sea Bass • Blowfish • Bluefish • Flounder (Winter Flounder) • Fluke (Summer Flounder) • Kingfish • Pollock • Scup (Porgy) • Striped Bass • Triggerfish • Weakfish

Freshwater Species
Catfish • Largemouth Bass • Smallmouth Bass • Panfish—Bluegill and Yellow Perch • Trout—Brook, Brown and Rainbow • Walleye

Chapter 2. Hot Spots 35
Staten Island • Rockaway Inlet • Jamaica Bay • Reynolds Channel • Jones Inlet • Zachs Bay • Fire Island Inlet/Great South Bay • Moriches Bay/Inlet • Shinnecock Bay/Inlet/Canal • Great Peconic Bay • Montauk Point • Gardiners Island/Bay • Peconic Bay/Shelter Island • Orient Point • North Fork/North Side • Shoreham Pipeline • Mt. Sinai Harbor • Port Jefferson Harbor • Nissequogue River • Smithtown Bay • Smithtown Artificial Reef • Huntington Bay • Matinecock Point • Hempstead Harbor • Prospect Point • Execution Light • Western Sound

Chapter 3. Montauk—A Surfcaster's Paradise 89
Montauk • Up Front • North Side • Shagwong • South Side—East • South Side—West

Chapter 4. Local Long Island Wrecks 95
South Wreck • SS Continent • 59 Pounder • Dodger
• Drumelzier • Shagri-La • Three Sisters • Eureka
• Iberia • The Immaculata • Long Island Sound Barges

Chapter 5. Freshwater Hot Spots 111

Chapter 6. Ramps, Beach Access 117

Chapter 7. Resources: Party Boats, Charter Boats, and Tackle Shops 129

Index 141

DEDICATION

I would like to dedicate this book to my mom. Ever since I was a young boy, she made sure I had a fishing rod and hooks—the real deal or makeshift, plus the transportation needed to get to the fishing hot spots. I remember fishing for catfish with a safety pin at Byron Lake State Park in Oakdale. Snapper fishing off the Islip Town Docks and best of all, being able to play hooky from school on the opening day of trout season at the Nissequogue River.

My mom passed away on May 21st 2004, a little more than three weeks after Peter Burford asked me to write this book. She was thrilled that her little boy had grown up, was doing something he loved—Editor of *The Fisherman* Magazine—and now an offer to write a book. Without her help as I grew, I would never have been as successful as I am today.

I love you mom, and miss you with every passing day.

ACKNOWLEDGMENTS

Special Thanks

There are so many people that need to be thanked the list would be pages long. First up would be my loving wife Kathie, who has supported me every day of 25-plus years of marriage. My three loving daughters: Lauren—my big girl, Ashley—the tall one, and Brittany—my "catcher," were there to encourage me throughout the writing. My sisters, Joan and Betty, always kept me in line in my younger years when Mom was working, and for this I thank them—although I know they hated me for it. They also helped me as I grew, with support and guidance (nagging).

There were others—my publisher at *The Fisherman*, and good friend, Fred Golofaro. Without Fred's help and tutelage in my earlier writing years, I would not be the writer I am today. To all of my friends and co-writers from the New York Metropolitan Outdoor Press Association—the old guys, who I look up to in the writing world. Special thanks to Ken Schultz for the knowledge and information gained from his *Fishing Encyclopedia*. And fellow outdoor writers on Long Island and tackle-shop owners, without whose valuable knowledge this book could not have been completed. Special thanks to Capt. John Raguso, who helped with the inshore wreck area.

On a personal note, my best friend Rick Holmberg, who is always ready to fish, and is always around when needed. You're the best friend a guy could have.

And last, but certainly not least, my thanks to the Reina family of Rich Sr. and Rich Jr., owners of *The Fisherman* Magazine, who gave me the opportunity to become editor over 11 years ago.

—Tom Melton
Manorville, New York
June, 2005

1

THE FISH AND HOW TO CATCH THEM

SALTWATER SPECIES

Atlantic Cod
The Atlantic cod (*Gadus morhua*) is known locally as just plain cod. For years, the cod was the mainstay of the recreational fishery in the winter months, with solid action and fish over 40 pounds commonplace. Like many of our recreational species, over-fishing by commercial interests caused a decline in the cod stocks. Over the past several years, however, it appears cod is on the rise again—partly due to commercial closures.

Cod are easily recognizable by their three dorsal fins, two anal fins and whisker (barbel) under the chin. They vary in color from red to gray, with phases of each color differing as well. For the gray phase, cod can be black to brownish gray to greenish, according to *McClane's Fishing Encyclopedia*. In the red phase, fish will be reddish-brown to orange to brick red. In my experience, most of the cod I have caught have been in the light brown to green coloring.

Angling technique for cod is simple—drop down a hunk of clam bait, let it sit, and then wait for a tug. Okay, it's not that easy! Cod angling takes patience, and the ability to hold a bait motionless, even in turbulent seas. The ability to free-spool a bait, allowing it to appear as motionless as possible, will increase your score at the day's end at least three-fold. For cod, beefier, heavy-duty sticks are the recommended rods. A rod in the 20- to 40-pound class, with a slow taper and solid backbone, is best. Some anglers call cod rods "broom sticks" due to their lack of sensitivity. A good quality reel in the 4/0 or larger size class is needed as well. You need to have at least 300 to 400 yards of 30- to 40-pound test mono, or a braid in similar pound strengths.

For terminal gear, cod can be a "bait and wait" game, or you can jig them. Cod love herring, and if the fish finder is marking bait, throw on a large six- to nine-inch Crippled Herring jig that can be jigged amongst the bait schools. If no bait is showing, it is best to anchor up on structure, and then use clam bait, held fast to the bottom by a sinker in the 10 to 20-ounce class.

Cod is one of the few fish that virtually every person, who either remotely or avidly eats fish, will love. They can be served in a variety of dishes, but are best known when served "fish & chips" style, breaded and fried, with a side order of fries. In fact, most of the fish that is offered at fast-food restaurants is cod.

Blackfish (Tautog)

Although Long Islanders call it a blackfish, it is actually a tautog (*Tautoga onitis*). A blackfish also goes by other names—tog and white chin as well. Blackfish are members of the Labridae family of wrasses, which numbers over 50 species!

Although blackfish are not known as the hardest fighters, they are stubborn, and react quickly to being hooked by heading into safe cover—usually rocks! Once in the rocks, these stubborn fish can be landed only by patient anglers.

Blackfish inhabit Long Island waters from January to June, and then again in the fall, from October through the end of year. There will be a smattering of fish caught in the summer, but for the most part, the better runs are in the months with cooler water temperatures.

Blackfish are usually found around some form of structure. On the South Shore, any of the bridge abutments, artificial reefs or mussel beds will hold fish. Moving up to the North Shore, virtually every rock in the Sound will have life where blackfish are concerned. Anglers working the shallow 15- to 20-foot depths early on score well. As the season progresses, blacks move to deeper, colder water.

The main diet of a blackfish is crabs. By using green or hermit crabs, anglers are almost guaranteed success. Other baits can be used, but are not as productive as fiddler crabs and sand worms.

For rigs, a simple one or two-hook set up is preferred. I like one hook as it leaves less chance that upon hookup, the second hook getting lodged in the rubble, forcing a break-off, a lost rig and an aggravated angler! Place the hook about four to six inches above the sinker and you are set. Keep the leader relatively short—10 to 15 inches. You also might want to tie an overhand knot in the sinker leg. With this knot, if the sinker does become stuck, the line weakness caused by the overhand knot will cause the line to break, losing only the sinker, and not the hook, and possibly the fish.

In choosing a rod and reel, be prepared for war where blackfish are concerned. These scrappy fighters know exactly what to do when hooked—head for cover and hold on! A stout rod rated for 20 to 40 pounds, and in the 7- to 8-foot length, will work great. I like the Castaway Muskie Rod, which is slightly smaller at 6-foot, 9 inches, but has the backbone of a football lineman! Match this rod to a good revolving-spool reel like the Calcutta 400 or Penn 975, and you have one tough rig! For line, braid gets the nod here as the sensitivity gives the angler a great advantage when feeling for the tap of a tog. And, with the braid, once hooked, the fish has very little chance of getting back into the rocks due to braid's lack of stretch. I also use a 40-pound fluorocarbon leader.

Black Sea Bass

Black sea bass (*Centropristis striata*), known locally just as sea bass, are terrific table fare, but must be kept cool after catching, as their flesh will ruin fast in the warm sun. Sea bass also must be handled with care after catching. The spiny dorsal fin of a sea bass, dead or alive, will puncture human skin with ease, causing a painful wound.

Sea bass are found locally on any piece of bottom structure from Sheepshead Bay to Montauk. Although anglers will catch them on the North Shore Sound waters, they appear in greater numbers on the South Shore. Sea bass will arrive on our inshore waters in May, with best action lasting until late June. The action picks up again in the late fall, November and December. Over the course of the winter months, sea bass will be found, along with the porgies, on deeper wrecks and pieces 200 feet down.

Despite having fairly large mouths, sea bass are still pretty good at pecking off your bait if you are not careful. And, with large mouths, they have also been known to grab a larger hunk of clam belly, or whole fish meant for a larger predator like stripers or codfish.

A typical hi/lo rig, similar to the porgy rig, works best. The big difference between the two is hook size. For sea bass you'll want to use hooks in the 2/0 through 4/0 size, with a leader about two to three feet between the hooks. The rod and reel outfit will be in the 12 to 20-pound class inshore, with 20 to 40-pound class offshore, due to heavier weights. Sea bass can also be jigged with tins, but best action is with standard squid or clam baits.

If you catch a good old-fashioned humpback sea bass, this would be a male in the over five-pound class. These males will have a pronounced lump just behind the head, and the coloration of these fish is absolutely beautiful, with rays of purple, blue and red tinges.

Most sea bass in our inshore waters will tend to be in the one to two-pound range, while on the offshore grounds, fish to three to five pounds will be more common. When fishing for blackfish in the fall, sea bass and porgies could round out the catch, making for a great smorgasbord at the dinner table.

Blowfish—Northern Puffer

My first blowfish (*Sphoeroides maculates*) was caught while fishing off the Bay Shore Marina Dock. The year was about 1967, and my mom had dropped me off for a day of fishing. Complete with peanut butter and jelly sandwiches, a Thermos of milk and my rod, reel and clams, I was set. The tug I felt at the end of my line was different than the snapper and fluke I had caught before, and indeed what greeted me after landing was a sight to see. When I went to unhook it, it blew up to twice its size and scared me to death. After all, I was only eight years old, and had never caught one! I ran to the marina with fish in tow, where the owner unhooked it for me. After getting an explanation of this fish I was able to unhook one on my own—but I also learned to watch out for the teeth, which are actually bones of the upper and lower jaw and not really teeth. But then again, they look like teeth to me!

Blowfish were a fish every angler could catch at will, every time they hit one of the local bays around Long Island. That was then, and this is 2005! Blowfish have returned, but not nearly in the numbers they once were.

Blowfish can be caught on virtually any bait, and are found around docks, pilings, and bridge abutments. Some of the deeper holes in the bays are also home to puffers. They are easily identified by the sandpaper-like skin, white belly, and the inevitable blow-up feature once landed.

For angling purposes, the blowfish, and kingfish (which we'll discuss later) can be caught on the same gear as winter flounder.

Bluefin Tuna

Bluefin tuna, especially the smaller 30 to 70 pounders we find on our inshore wrecks, are deep blue on top, blending to silver along their sides and bellies. Bluefin tuna have two dorsal fins, one anal fin, plus numerous dorsal and anal finlets. The bluefin is built for speed, and will really test an angler's skills, especially on 20 to 30-pound class stand-up outfits. Bluefin begin to appear off the Long Island coast in late June, with the schoolies staying in the 15- to 25-fathom areas until late October and some of the larger specimens hanging out until Thanksgiving, if the bait and water temps are to their liking. Anglers can troll or chunk bluefins with herring, butterfish, mackerel, and squid key baits.

Bluefish

Blues are the hardest fighting fish of the inshore species. I consider the bluefish (*Pomatomus saltatrix*) the mad dog! Blues, also called snappers (young of the year fish), cocktails (two to three months) and choppers (fish over 10 pounds), are aggressive eating machines that eat until they are full, spill their guts, and then eat some more. They literally will eat until there is no food left to eat—tide after tide. They will ravage any bait in the water, and in fact will eat their own if they get in the way. Countless times, striper anglers have come back with a bass with no tail, thanks to a chopper looking for an easy meal.

The only drawback to the bluefish is its taste. Although some anglers like blues—like my neighbor John Blanco, who eats them as fast I can catch them—they are best saved for grilling on the barbecue or smoking, which tends to curb their harsh taste. One tip to make a tastier bluefish is to bleed the fish immediately after it is caught.

Bluefish can be targeted from the surf, boat or pier. In the early stages of the year, blues will begin showing on the West End of the South Shore, on the heels of the mackerel schools making their way up the coast. As they hit Long Island, bluefish enter every bay and harbor, wreaking havoc on every angler, and every fish. At times, blues will be so plentiful you cannot get through them to target any other species. By June, blues will be in the Sound, but still on the small side—one to three pounds. By August, choppers in the 10-plus pound class will become a common sight.

Blues are a tackle-shop owner's best friend. No other fish will have anglers buying tackle over and over again, day after day, than a bluefish. These tackle-busting brutes will destroy gear with hard fought runs that will leave anglers in awe at their strength and determination.

The best method for blues for the boating crowd is chunk baits—bunker and mackerel are the favorites. Although blues will jump all over live bait such as bunker or porgy, chunks will account for a steady pick of action. For the surf angler, nothing beats a good old-fashioned Charlie Graves, Hopkins, Kastmaster or Crippled Herring tin, or Andrus bucktail. The only problem is that after several fish, the bucktail hair on the Andrus and Charlie Graves styles will be long gone. For this reason, if the blues are ravaging, use one of the jigs with no hair. If the catch ratio stays the same, you're home; if not, it's back to the first two, and a lot of lost hair. But hey, that's the price we pay for success!

When peanut bunker begin to show along the South Shore surf in late October and November, blues can be caught on small topwater metal-lip swimmers as well as Gibbs Pencil Poppers.

For the kids, nothing beats the fun of snappers, which are young-of-the-year blues. Snappers will begin showing in late June, but will not be able to be hooked until late July. From this point on, snappers, depending on the weather, will stay around until late September. Snappers can be caught from virtually any dock on the North or South Shores. Small tins, or the old bobber, hook and spearing set-up, are all you need for non-stop fun.

For blues, like blackfish, stout tackle is the way to go. These fish will put any angler's tackle to the test, so smooth drags and quality rods are a must. The same rod you use for blackfish will work well on blues in the 10-plus pound class. However, if the fish you are targeting are the smaller ones, drop down one notch to a 12 to 25-

pound class rod and reel outfit. For line, I like mono over braid here as I feel mono does not break as easy on the sharp teeth or dorsal fins of ravaging blues.

Moving to the boat, an egg sinker of adequate weight and 7/0 Gamakatsu hook is best. The super-sharp Gamakatsu hooks make hook sets a breeze, even in the tough mouth of a bluefish. To set up the rig, put the egg sinker on your standing line, and then tie in a barrel swivel. Next, tie on a 30-inch length of fluorocarbon of at least 40-pound test, and then the hook. The only real difference between this rig and the surfcaster's rig is that surfcasters will add a float between the hook and barrel swivel to keep the bait off the bottom and away from crabs.

False Albacore and Bonito

A false albacore is actually a little tunny (*Euthynnus alletteratus*), and can be found in and around the South Shore and North Shore inlets and harbors in the fall. Primarily feeding on small baitfish, false albies will wreak havoc on baitfish, and can be seen slashing through the water. Albies are very distinguishable in that they have wavy, somewhat vertical lines above the lateral line. For angling purposes, most of the action will be on the fly rod, with small anchovy flies working best. When targeting albies, don't rush the school. Stay up-current and allow the boat to drift towards the melee.

The Atlantic bonito (*Sarda sarda*) is similar in shape to the albie, but has lines moving from the head in a slightly upward pattern towards the tail. They, too, can be found around inlets and harbors, as well as the offshore wrecks and deep-water fathom curve lines. Tactics for bonito are similar to those used on albies, but bonito can also be caught with butterfish baits or on the troll with small birds or feathers.

Flounder (Winter)

Winter flounder (*Pseudopleuronectes americanus*) are smaller than their cousins, the summer flounder (fluke). The winter flounder is a right-handed fish, meaning that as the fish lies flat on the bottom, its eyes are on the right side of his body. The fish is so-named "winter" due to its preference for cool weather. They arrive early in the season, and then depart the inshore bays as the waters warm. Usually by the beginning of July, the bays are devoid of winter flounder. As the fall approaches, flounder will reappear, usually around the end of September, with better catches towards the seasons end, from late October and into December. Winter flounder are best found in the shallow bays around Long Island.

Flounder action can be best achieved on light tackle rods and reels, with light line as well. For starters, I like conventional gear as it offers more control and the ability to whip a stray fluke or striper in the early going. A rod in the 6½ to 7-foot length, rated for 12 to 15-pound test, and matched to a good quality revolving spool reel like the Abu-Garcia 6500 will suffice. On the line end, even though braid has hit the fishing world like a storm, I still prefer monofilament in 10-pound test. The 10-pound line still has a fairly thin diameter, which will work well, allowing lighter sinkers to hold bottom.

On the terminal end, here is where it gets tricky. Some like it plain and simple, some like fanciness. For me, I meet halfway in between. When I flounder fish, I use a simple two-hook setup, and add a chartreuse curly-tail grub over the snell in the hook. I have seen yellow, red, purple and shocking pink used, but I like my chartreuse. As for who catches more—I really think that is up to the angler, and not the color of his grub.

Flounder are primarily lazy bottom feeders that adore sandworms or bloodworms, clams and mussels. Although most early-season fish are loaded with grass shrimp, they are also fond of krill, a small shrimp-like crustacean.

Along with typical baits, fluke anglers should bring along chum and whole bank mussels. These two ingredients will aid in bringing flounder to your baited hook, enhancing your catch. Another key is some form of pounding device. Whether it is a long pole, sash weights, or you use your chum pot—banging the bottom works wonders. In doing this, small bait and clam pieces are flushed out, enticing the flounder into more voracious feeding.

Flounder (Summer)

Like the winter flounder, the summer flounder (*Paralichthys dentatus*) spends most of the time hunkered down to the bottom, hiding in shelter, waiting for an easy meal. The main difference between winter and summer flounder lies in the tooth department. Summer flounder (called fluke in our area) have large mouths and a set of teeth that will rip and tear most baitfish, while flounder have relatively small mouths and small teeth. A fluke is also a left-handed fish, meaning the eyes are on the left side of its body. Fluke also grow quite a bit large than winter flounder, and at times can push the teen class. The late Charlie Nappi caught the world record, which weighed 22 pounds, 7 ounces, off Montauk. Most fluke in our waters, however, will be in the two- to six-pound class. Another difference between the two flounder is the time period they arrive in the Long Island waters, as fluke will be here throughout the summer, and into fall.

For targeting fluke, most action is done with a boat. Although they can be caught from the various piers and the inlet jetties, the better action is had on a boat—party, charter or private. Anglers will catch fluke in the bays in anywhere from one foot of water to 10 to 15 feet, while ocean anglers will fish in upwards of 80 to 100 feet, depending on the time of year, and where the bait is staging.

Fluke will begin showing in our waters off the East End and North Fork the first week of May. Some incidental small fish will be caught in late April on the South Shore, but the real run usually begins out east. On the North Fork, anglers will also see larger fish for the most part, as the fish follow squid into inshore waters. Following the North Fork, the East End-Montauk waters will heat up next, followed by the South Shore, and then the North Shore by mid to late June.

For fluke on the inshore grounds, a 6½ to 7-foot rod, rated for 10 to 15 pound line and an Ambassadeur reel spooled with either 15-

pound mono or 20-pound braid will work well. For ocean action, where heavier sinkers are usually needed, go with a slightly heavier outfit in the 15 to 20-pound class. Spinning rods and reels should remain home when targeting fluke in favor of conventional gear.

Rigs will vary from simple three-way set-ups, where the hook is approximately 36 inches from the three-way, while the sinker is on a short trace of two to three inches. On this set-up, spearing and a squid strips are the main baits. Fluke however adore any strip bait, including sea robin, bluefish, bunker, or the belly of their own.

Anglers will also target fluke using artificial lures like bucktails, silver balls, and so forth. These can be fished with an additional hook approximately 20 inches higher on the standing line or by themselves. The big difference is presentation. When using bait, allow the rig to slide along the bottom, lifting occasionally. For the artificial, the bucktail must be kept moving in a slight jigging motion. The bucktail should also be tipped with a single spearing or strip of the aforementioned baits. For the most part, the bucktail style can only be used in water less than 25 feet in depth.

Kingfish
In our area, the northern kingfish (*Menticirrhus saxatilis*) is found on the inshore grounds around docks and bridge abutments. Actually a member of the whiting family, the northern is one of four *Menticirrhus* whitings. Our kingfish is only found on the Atlantic coast, from Maine to Florida.

Like blowfish, kingfish used to be around in large quantities, but over the years their stocks have diminished. Kingfish can be found along any of the South Shore docks during the summer months. They will begin showing around the end of June, and then stick around until late September. Kingfish are a great fish for the table, although most anglers prefer to use them as live bait for striped bass.

Kingfish are best caught with small pieces of clam or squid, with a typical hi-lo rig and number 4 or 6 hook working well.

Simply drop the rig to the bottom, and use slight lifts, similar to the technique for flounder fishing. Check your bait often, as crabs in the shallows can become quick bait stealers. Kingfish are scrappy fighters, which make them great quarry for the kids as well. For tackle, a light rod and reel outfit, either spinning or baitcasting, in the 8 to 12-pound class will work fine.

Pollock

Pollock (*Pollachius virens*), like the Atlantic cod, is a staple for bottom fishermen along the East coast. The pollock is the most active of all the cod family, which makes it a prime target for anglers. Pollock will readily take jigs, and in all water depths.

Pollock, like their cousin the cod, have a barbell located on the underside of the lower jaw. As pollock age, the barbell on pollock will usually disappear. The main difference between the two is that on the pollock, the lower jaw projects past the upper jaw, while the lateral line is virtually straight. The pollock prefers rocky structure, and prefers depths slightly shallower than cod and haddock.

For tackle, stout rods in the 20- to 40-pound class, similar to cod rods, will work well. Any good revolving-spool reel capable of holding between 300 and 400 yards of 30-pound test is best. Pollock will usually be found in the same haunts as cod, therefore the terminal tackle is similar: single or double hooks, or some form of four- to 12-ounce jig fished vertically in the water column.

Scup

Scup (*Stenotomus chrysops*), better known in our area as porgies, are one of the hardest fighters we encounter. As the late Scott Simons, editor of *The Fisherman Magazine* once said, "If porgies grew to 20 pounds, they would be the most sought-after gamefish on the East coast." These little guys, ½ to 3 pounds, will fight like the dickens when hooked, making for an enjoyable fish to catch for both young and adult anglers.

Porgies are a schooling fish found in the inshore waters in the summer, from Massachusetts to Virginia. In the winter months they head offshore, where party boat anglers can catch them off the deep-water wrecks over 200 feet down.

Porgies are the favorite of the party boat clan, with anglers filling buckets at will during what is almost always non-stop action. In fact, there will be times when anglers will actually stop fishing due to tired arms!

Porgies are best caught on lighter tackle, with a rod rated for 10 to 15 pounds working just fine. However, if you plan on fishing the winter offshore grounds, you will need to beef it up a bit due to the amount of lead you'll need to hit bottom and stay there. Back on the inshore grounds, most times you will be fishing with between one and five ounces, depending on current and water depth.

For baits, clams are best, but porgies will readily take sea worms and squid. Porgies are also one of the premier bait stealers you will ever meet. A quick peck, and your bait is gone. You had better be quick on the hook set, or it will be a long day at the rail. With porgies being a schooling fish, however, even if you do miss one and he gets a free meal, there will be plenty more for the taking.

A typical two-hook, hi/lo rig is all that you need for porgies. Use a sproat-style hook in size 1/0 or slightly smaller, leadered from dropper loops spaced 12 to 15 inches apart. Tie in a loop under this rig for the sinker.

Porgies are great for the kids too. They are relatively easy to catch despite being bait stealers, and will have the kids reeling in fish until they are tired. And, believe me, they will not get bored on this fishing trip.

Striped Bass

Striped bass (*Marone saxitillis*) is the most sought after gamefish on the Long Island coast. Anglers will target stripers with light tackle, trolling gear and standard bottom gear with one thing in mind—to bring home a trophy fish for the wall, or for dinner. And, they will target them by boat or shore, day or night!

Around the middle of April, stripers will begin showing on the North Shore, towards Manhasset and Little Neck bays. The first body of fish will be in the school variety—five to 10 pounds—but will quickly be replaced by fish in the low teens to 20-plus pound class. As April progresses, stripers will become a common sight in all North Shore harbors. At the same time, bass will cover the South Shore from Staten Island to Montauk, with fish from 10 to 50 pounds. Some of the better spots for stripers in the early going on the South Shore will include any of the bridges or inlets, plus the State Channel or Reynolds Channel.

Rich Tenreiro of Northeast Angling Productions caught this 52.9-pound bass while swimming a live bunker in Manhasset Bay.

From this point, and continuing throughout the year until after Thanksgiving, striped bass will be found in virtually every haunt around Long Island. How you catch them is up to the individual angler.

Tactics for Stripers

There are many ways to target striped bass, but if you want to score consistently with fish in the high 20- to 40-pound class, live bait is the way to go. On the North Shore, bunker is the prevalent bait, while South Shore sharpies will employ live eels, bergalls, kingfish, legal-sized flounder, porgies and blackfish. Moving towards the east end of the island, the live bait of choice is the slimy snake—eel. Although many large stripers will succumb to live baits, cut baits, worms and artificial lures will also account for action—and produce large fish as well.

For terminal rigging, live baits are best suited to a three-way rig or fish finder consisting of a leader, egg sinker and hook. The "Keep It Simple Stupid" (KISS) method is best used here. If you are fishing a harbor area, and bunker is on top, lose the weight and just allow the bait to swim naturally. There is nothing better than to have a lively bunker swimming on the surface, followed by a huge boil, and within seconds—CRASH—a bass mauls the bait.

For the light tackle and surf clan—where artificial lures and bucktails prevail—a leader of between 20 and 40 inches is used from the standing line, and then a duo-lock snap attaches the artificial lure to your leader. Surf anglers will use plugs, tins and bucktails from one to five ounces, while light-tackle anglers will use smaller offerings in the one-half to two-ounce range.

Other baits are employed for stripers including clam bellies, skimmer clams, blood and sandworms, and even strip baits from sea robins and fluke, along with squid. For these baits the three-way rig works best. What all anglers must realize is that stripers are like sharks without teeth. They will eat virtually anything in their paths, viciously attacking a meal at certain times. Although sometimes viewed as lethargic feeders, striped bass are not so much lethargic, as opportunistic. On the tackle end, your choice will depend on the method—fly, light tackle, surf, or boat—of action you choose. For most anglers, the boat action is tops, with surf second, light tackle third, and fly last.

For boaters, a rod in the six and a half to seven-foot length, rated for 20 to 40 pounds, will suffice. Match this to a good quality conventional reel like the Shimano Calcutta 400 or Penn 975 TLD and you're home free. On the line end, I like 20-pound test mono, but some instances call for going heavier, or at least using a heavy mono leader in the 40 to 60-pound rating. Kathy Kronuch, owner of Johnny's Tackle in Montauk, uses a 60-pound leader, which is sometimes eight feet long! This may be too long for some, but this lady wins more party boat pools than anyone I know!

Moving to surf, the main stick used will be an 11-foot graphite (Lamiglas GSB1321M blank), matched to a large-capacity spinning reel, capable of holding at least 300 yards of 20-pound test mono. Your budget will dictate the reel you choose. For the high-end angler, the two top surf reels are the Van Staal 300 and the Stella 8000 or 10000. These babies will set you back over $500. However, the old stand-by Penn 706Z or 704Z cannot be beat for longevity and ease of maintenance. These will only run you in the $100 range. For line, most anglers these days have made the switch to braid, and use a 30-pound braid with 40-pound leader.

Light tackle has also hit striper fishing like a storm. Here is where it really gets to be fun. Stripers in the teen to 20-plus pound class can be caught at virtually every bridge, dock piling, back bay and harbor. In fact, one such area—Manhasset Bay—sees anglers catch as many as 50 to 100 per tide when it's hot! For tackle, a six and a half to seven-foot spinning or conventional style outfit is the preferred choice. For me, I like the conventional set-up and use the same reel, an Ambassadeur 6500C, that I use floundering, and a six-foot, six-inch St. Croix rod rated as medium action, with a line rating of 10 to 20-pound test.

Last but not least—fly-fishing. For the fly guru, I checked in with Guy Zummo, one of Long Island's premier fly fishermen. Guy feels that a nine-weight, nine-foot, medium-action rod is the best overall choice when fishing the bays, inlets and along the North Shore. When working the ocean beaches, Montauk Point or casting oversized flies, a 10-weight rod works best.

Large arbor fly reels, capable of holding at least 150 yards of 30-pound test backing, are preferred for their fast line retrieval. An intermediate fly line and a 350 to 400-grain shooting head will be your primary fly lines. With these, you will be able to present your flies from the surface down to 15-feet deep. Complete your setup with a nine-foot tapered leader with a 15-pound test tippet. Use a 30-pound test shock tippet for trophy fish.

Triggerfish

According to Ken Schultz's *Fishing Encyclopedia*, triggerfish are in the *Balistidae* family, consisting of 40 species in 11 genera. They also have several characteristics that other species in our area do not possess. They have independently moving eyes, a leathery skin, which is void of a slime or mucus coating, and the most intriguing is the "trigger." The trigger allows the fish to erect its first spine of the dorsal, locking it in place. In doing this, the triggerfish can wedge itself between rocks and be virtually immovable.

Some queen triggers have been caught in our area, but we mostly catch the gray variety. Both can range as high as 12 to 13 pounds, although most anglers will battle fish in the two to six-pound class. The state record incidentally was caught in late August of 2001 and weighed in at 7.63 pounds.

In speaking with Gary Grunseich of Silly Lily Fishing Station in East Moriches, I learned that triggers inhabit the local buoy chains of Moriches Bay every summer and fall. To find them, simply pull up to a buoy and look down! With the water in the bay very clear in July and August, you will see them quite easily.

Rental stations are located on the north and south shores. This is Gary Grunseich's "Silly Lily," located in East Moriches.

After finding the triggers, anchor a short distance away and allow the boat to get fairly close the buoy. Drop some clam chum down, and you can catch them for quite some time with a simple two-hook tandem rig and clam bait.

On the jetties along the South Shore, the key is a float. Sounds silly, especially with rushing currents, but the best triggerfish action is 30 minutes before and after the high slack turn. When fishing this turn, the current is virtually non-existent.

The rig is simple: tie on a number 4 or 6 blackfish or Sproat hook. Approximately two-inches above the hook add in a rubber-core sinker, then about two feet above this a large snapper bobber (3-inch diameter). Lob the rig out away from the jetty a short distance, and then allow it to drift with the current. This set-up will allow the bait to get close to the bottom, yet stay out of the rocks, avoiding snags.

From the shore, a stout, an eight to nine-foot spinning rod with a fast taper, is best. This style will allow you to feel the bite, plus offer the backbone needed to lift the fish over the rocks. It will also allow for the stray striper, bulldog tog or bluefish to be landed.

For the boating angler, a simple six to seven-foot conventional or spinning outfit in the 12 to 15-pound class will suffice. Match either of these rods to a good quality reel with smooth drag, and you're set. On the line end, there is no need to get fancy. Monofilament in the 20-pound class will work fine.

Weakfish

Weakfish (*Cynoscion regalis*) begin showing in nets off the waters of Long Island in late March and early April. By late April, they have begun to flood the South Shore bays, Peconic Bay and Shinnecock Canal area. By mid-May, they begin showing off the Western Sound Harbor mouths and points. As the season progresses and the waters warm, the large weaks vacate the inshore waters, and are replaced by a smaller version, or summer run weaks. These are the fry of a good spawn.

Weakfish are rather easy to identify in our waters as no other fish is gifted with a fang, actually two, on their upper jaw. Weakfish are also colorful, with dark olive or greenish to greenish-blue on the dorsal surface. The sides display purple, blue, lavender, green and golden tinges.

Weakfish are a bit spooky, and will easily become line shy, or people shy if there is too much noise in the area. With this in mind, the better catches are usually made in the early morning, or after dark.

Weakfish can be caught with a variety of methods. The most popular is light tackle gear combined with soft artificial lures. Large jelly worms in grape and strawberry are favored, but anglers can readily catch their share using Fin-S Fish, Bass Assassins, Storm WildEye shads, and a plethora of other soft plastic baits. Depending on the current and water depth, leadheads in the one-quarter to one-ounce weight will be used in conjunction with the soft plastics. Small swimming plugs and poppers will also produce action, especially on the flats or in the early morning.

For the angler wishing to use bait, sand worms and squid strips are the best baits, but large tiderunner weaks over the 10-pound mark have been known to take live baits like snappers, bergalls, peanut and large bunker at will.

The typical weakfish rig for bait fishing involves a hi-lo rig with one hook about three inches off the bottom, while the second is another 12 to 15 inches higher than the first. This rig, tipped with the appropriate bait, will produce in all Long Island areas.

As for artificials, light line or a braid with fluorocarbon leader is the way to go. Start off with a small Spro barrel swivel on the line leading to your reel. I like Spro as the diameter is very small, and can be reeled in through the guides without damaging them. To the opposite end of the barrel, tie on a trace of 15 to 20-pound fluorocarbon approximately 15 to 20 inches in length. Tie the artificial directly, with no snap swivel.

Typical rod and reel outfits can range from a light-action freshwater type to a medium-weight baitcasting outfit in the 15 to 20-pound class. I prefer two outfits, depending on the area or method fishing. If I am probing the local docks after dark, I use a six to six and a half foot spinning rod rated for 10 to 14-pound and Shimano Stradic 2500, spooled with 20-pound braid. If I am boat fishing, I will go slightly heavier, 12 to 20 pound class, and switch to a baitcaster. The baitcast outfit will give you more control when battling a tiderunner in heavier currents or deeper water.

FRESHWATER SPECIES

Trout—Brook, Rainbow and Brown

For trout info, I hooked up with fellow Great South Bay Angler Club member, and the owner of Hooks and Brooks Guide Service (631-589-0065), Mark Malenovsky. Mark has been guiding for many years, and if one angler knows trout on Long Island, Mark is the guy!

According to Mark, brook trout are found in several waterways on Long Island—specifically the Connetquot, Carmens and Nissequogue areas. Although small waterways do hold a few, these are a minor fisheries compared to the big three in Suffolk County. In fact, virtually any creek that runs into Great South Bay, at one time, did contain a population of brookies. The New York City and Long Island Chapters of Trout Unlimited have been working with officials, garnering grant funds, and trying to bring back brookies to Long Island. As of 2004, brook trout on Long Island is strictly catch and release, except when fishing Connetquot River or Caleb Smith State parks.

Brookies (*Salvelinus fontinalis*) are easily identifiable by the red spots with blue aureoles on the sides. The caudal fin is only slightly forked, and in fact appears almost square.

As for rainbows, these are stocked in virtually every stream on the island, and almost all of these streams have a native population as well. For best action however, the Nissequogue and Connetquot rivers, due to their high concentration of stocking, are the best locations. Upper Lake in Yaphank and Laurel Lake in Mattituck are other options that hold fish.

Rainbows (*Oncorhynchus mykiss*), according to *Ken Schultz's Fishing Encyclopedia*, are distinguishable by the reddish pink band along each side about midline which may range from faint to radiant. The lower sides will be silver, possibly fading to pure white.

For brown trout (*Salmo trutta*), the best spots would be the Connetquot and Carmens rivers, with sea runs available in any of the tidal sections of these two. The Carmens also has good action below Southaven Park—this being the tidal section. Laurel Lake in Mattituck is another hot spot. Last on the list would be any of the local lakes in Nassau and Suffolk counties where the New York State DEC stocks two-year-old browns. As the list changes each year, it is best to call DEC for dates, amounts and stocking locations.

For angling, fly fishing is the best bet choice. According to Mark Malenovsky, the three flies to focus on would be a parachute Adams in sizes 12 to 20, the Gold Ribbed Hare's Ear nymph, in size 12 to 18, and the Muddler Minnow streamer, which can be fished on top like a grasshopper or fishing it like a minnow by adding weight. For this Mark likes a size 6 to 10.

For those less inclined to pick up the long wand, typical light tackle spinning gear will account for banner days on the water. Try standard garden earthworms for solid results. Fish these on a float rig or unweighted. Small jigs used for crappie also work well, while any in-line spinner like Mepps or Rooster tails will take their fair share also. In the spoon department, small Cleo or Kastmasters in gold or silver are solid performers. Keep the lures light, $\frac{1}{16}$ to $\frac{1}{4}$-ounce. When working the tidal areas for larger trout, small Rapala or other jerk baits will account for bigger fish.

Catfish (Brown Bullhead)

Catfish species number over 2200 worldwide! However, the catfish we encounter most is the brown bullhead (*Ameriurus nebylosus*) Despite being high on the list of targeted species, catfish are not a heavily targeted species on Long Island. Catfish are found in the lakes of Staten Island, especially Wolfs Pond. Moving up island, cats will be caught in Lake Ronkonkoma and the Peconic River-Upper Mill areas.

For Long Island anglers, we see mostly brown bullheads in our region. Although there have been reports of black and yellow, they are few and far between. Bullheads are caught both day and night, however better action can be had after the sun goes down.

Cats can be caught recreationally three ways—noodling, setline and rod and reel. Noodling is more of a Southern tradition, in which the angler feels under large logs and such, and then when the cat—usually a 40-plus-pounder—grabs his arm, he pulls him out of the cover . . . No thanks, I'll pass on that one! Setline is more of a commercial-type fishery where anglers set lines out, then come back later at night, or another day to retrieve their catch. Rod and reel angling can be done in our waters, and in my opinion is the most sporting way to catch catfish.

For the most part, Long Island waters will not see bullheads over the 10-pound class. Use a light spinning rod, rated for 6 to 8 or 8 to 14-pound test. As bullheads are in the murkier waters, line can be in the 15-pound class, without the fear of a bullhead being line shy. Keep in mind to set your drag or the heavier line can snap your rod.

For bait, catfish can be caught on standard earthworms fished on the bottom, or just off. Other very good baits would be any cut fish—shad, herring, bluegill etc. If the cut bait is found in the waters you are fishing, all the better.

Largemouth Bass

Out of all the fish I catch over the course of a single season, no one fish thrills me more than the largemouth bass (*Micropterus salmoides*). Largemouth bass action on Long Island, in my opinion, is second to none in the state of New York. Sure, you may catch more fish in Lake Ontario, or the Finger Lakes, but, as for size, Long Island offers anglers the chance at a true five-plus pounder more than anywhere else. And, in fact, several fish over eight pounds, plus more than enough ten- pounders have been caught in recent years to believe there might be a State Record fish living on Long Island.

Largemouth bass can be caught in virtually every lake on the island. Although our season for the most part does get started until the first Saturday in June, we can catch fish right up until the year's end.

For tackle, I like to go heavy as bass will definitely head for cover, and live in cover whenever possible. In most of our lakes, trees, bushes, lily pads and more will make landing a trophy difficult at best. Stick with a rod rated for 12 to 18 pound test, and forget the light line here. In fact, on my jig rod, I use 30-pound Power Pro braid, while my spinnerbait rod uses 20-pound Power

The author with his favorite species—largemouth bass!

Pro. Both have a trace of 25 to 40-pound fluorocarbon leader tied in at the terminal end. The only time I go lighter is when worming, and even then I never go below 10-pound test. I prefer conventional reels in the 4.9:1 or 6.1:1 ratios.

For artificial lures, soft plastic worms fished slowly on the bottom, or dragged through lily pads, will work well. Jigs (I prefer blue with blue trailers), spinnerbaits, crankbaits and stickbaits however, will also account for solid action throughout the year. In fact, I had my largest ever, an estimated nine-plus pounder, on a small chartreuse spinnerbait several years ago while fishing Southaven Park in Yaphank.

Smallmouth Bass

Long Island is not known for smallmouth bass (*Micropterus dolomieui*), but they can be caught in the waters of Lake Ronkonkoma and Fort Pond. The climate around much of Long Island does not offer the environment that a smallmouth prefers—cooler water and rocky terrain.

The smallmouth bass—actually a sunfish like its brethren, the largemouth—is a feisty fish, which offers anglers spirited runs, and a stubbornness similar to the saltwater striped bass. They will readily take most artificial lures, especially ones that replicate a crawfish—the main diet of most smallmouth, and another reason they are not overly abundant on Long Island as crawfish are not either.

Due to their preference for open water and clear lakes, lighter tackle is used, and sometimes preferred. A light tackle rod rated for six to eight-pound test, or even an ultra-light in the four to six-pound class, is best suited for these sunfish. The best lure for smallies is a hair jig or soft-bodied plastic-legged jig.

Panfish—Bluegill and Yellow Perch

Panfish are typically smaller fish, that are very easy to catch, and can be quite prolific in most bodies of water. For Long Island, any of the local ponds will hold bluegills and yellow perch. Both are easily caught on worm baits and can be a blast for the youngsters.

Panfish are probably one of the first fish a young child will encounter. A small spinning rod or closed face rod and reel combo is the best starter set. Place a float approximately 12 inches above a number 6 or 8 hook baited with a worm, and the kids will be catching all day long.

As for eating, they are very good on the table, and replenish their stocks very quickly so over fishing rarely occurs. Bluegills are usually found close to shore in less than two feet of water. Yellow perch are found primarily in lakes or ponds offering virtually any bottom—muck, sand or gravel. They are not hard fighters, but when caught on light tackle will put up a spirited fight. Perch are also readily available on the local lakes in the winter when ice fishing.

Walleye

The walleye (*Stizostedion vitreum*) is the largest member of the perch family, attaining sizes of up to 20 pounds. In our area, two to four-pound fish are common. Anything over five pounds is great, while a fish of eight pounds or larger is a true trophy by any state's standards. On Long Island, walleye are only found in two bodies of water according to Charles Guthrie, Regional Fisheries Manager for Region One, New York State Department of Environmental Conservation. Walleye have been stocked in Lake Ronkonkoma and Fort Pond, with annual and bi-annual stockings of 10,000 and 4,000 fish respectively. Chart feels the walleye fishery is beginning to move. The fish is a long lived fish, where a 10-year-old fish is not uncommon. Since the stocking program only began in '94, with a limited number, and really started taking off in '96, we are only just approaching 10-year old fish.

Walleye are generally found in schools, and near the bottom of the lake. They are more of a nighttime feeder, and will readily take any live bait like shiners or minnows, but will also succumb to artificial lures that resemble small baitfish.

Typical gear for walleye is similar bass tackle. Use a six to six and a half foot rod, rated for 10 to 18 pound test for throwing crankbaits and minnow style lures. For lighter grubs and soft plastics, go with a slightly lighter spinning rod in the eight to 12-pound class. Any good quality reel filled with six to 12-poud test mono will work fine, however the newer braids will allow you to work around heavy cover, and still get a fish out.

2
HOT SPOTS

STATEN ISLAND

For saltwater fans, the south side of Staten Island offers ample access for beach anglers, as well as boatmen. As in any area you fish, local knowledge is always best. With this said, Staten Island is best fished with the help of Brian Flynn, owner of Biggies Bait and Tackle (718-966-9206).

According to Brian, there are three piers on Staten Island, and all offer parking for anglers. The first pier, located just minutes from the shop on Page Avenue, is Sharrot Pier. Sharrot Pier is easily reachable off Hyland Blvd, and is probably one of the better spots to take a youngster. The pier plays host to good porgy action in the spring, with fluke mixing in as well. As the summer rolls in, however, the kids can catch snappers all day long.

Brian Flynn of Biggies Bait and Tackle on Staten Island is a big weakfish fan, shown by his smile after catching this 5-pounder.

The next pier is the South Beach Pier, located off Midland Avenue, near Father Capedonno Street. This pier will see better action on fluke, with stripers and blues making an appearance as well.

Moving to the beach scene, the best spot for anglers would be the bottom of Suguin Avenue. This area is closest to the main shipping channels that surround Staten Island. A good caster can easily reach the 45-foot depths, or at least work the sloop, where baitfish and predators will stack up on various tides. (The sloop is the area where the water rapidly descends from shallow to deep. Predators will often slide up and down this area in search of an easy meal.) In the spring, school bass will quickly be replaced by cows upwards of 40 pounds. The best baits here are clams or chunks of bunker, or live eels after dark.

Great Kills Park is a favorite area for surfcasters as it holds bait virtually all year long—especially peanut bunker, which is a favorite of blues and bass. According to Brian, Great Kills Park and Gateway

National Park are the best surf spots on the island. In the spring, weakfish and bass will be the norm, while the summer sees chopper blues. As the fall approaches, bass and blues will re-enter the area, feasting before heading north and south for the winter months. Within Gateway is Crooks Point, another hot spot. (Be aware that for this area you will need a permit to park.)

There are many areas for boaters, all within an easy ride from Great Kills Harbor. For starters, Brian likes the area in front of Princes Bay—known to locals as the "Dental Works" for some unknown reason. This area will hold quality weakfish action in September, with live snappers accounting for weaks over the five-pound mark. In the spring, and again in early fall, the area outside the harbor near the West Bank Lighthouse will see solid action on school bass. Here anglers can enjoy topwater action as bass after bass crash plugs.

For bottom fishermen, the islands of Hoffman and Swinburne, located between Ambrose Channel and Staten Island, will see good action on blackfish, porgies and seas bass throughout the year. The islands also host good action along the banks for stripers.

Moving away from Staten Island, anglers with seaworthy boats in the 18-foot-plus class can fish Ambrose Channel. This area is home to super fluke action from May through the season's end.

NORTON'S POINT

In the 1970s, when weakfish were in abundance, anglers headed for this hotspot in droves. Each summer anglers would have a blast with yellowfins whether from the surf or by boat. Although weakfish action has tapered off compared to that timeframe, there are still opportunities worth to exploring.

Located between Gravesend and Lower New York Bay, in sight of the Coney Island Lighthouse, Norton's Point is part of the Gateway National Recreation Area and is a favorite destination for West End anglers. Whether you fish via boat or shore, this area will have your rod bending on almost every trip. To access Nortons

Point, anglers need to head due west from Rockaway Inlet for approximately five miles. Nortons Point is located at N40-34.686 W74-00.793. For shorebound anglers, access is by way for Gateway National Recreation area.

The area is made up of flats, ledges, rips and strong current, which attract bass, fluke, blues, weakfish and more. For starting points, the Coney Island Flats is an especially super area for fluke during the summer. From June to August, anglers bouncing bucktails and plastic jigs tipped with spearing, sand eels or squid strips do a fine job on quality fluke. During the spring and fall, anglers dunking worms will produce enough flounder for dinner, making for a pleasant day.

Despite the good winter and summer flounder action, anglers that fish Nortons will really be here for one thing—the fabulous gamesters of the West End. Stripers, blues and weakfish will all be on the radar screen. Diamond jigs without the tubes will work well for all three species when jigged off the bottom. With the area seeing a solid amount of current, Ava 27, 47 and 67 Diamond jigs will all produce. To lessen the drag during times of strong current—mid-tide phase—lose the tube and fish the hook bare, or with a trailer of porkrind.

ROCKAWAY INLET/REEF

Rockaway Inlet is the first inlet for anglers fishing the Long Island area from the Jersey shore and points south. The inlet is wide, safe, and offers great action on both tides. For shorebound casters, the Breezy Point area, at the tip of Rockway Inlet at the end of Rockaway Beach, offers some of the finest action with striped bass, blues and weaks from May throughout the fall.

For boaters, using live bunker, kingfish or eels should account for a bass or two, especially on the night tides. For bottom bouncers, Dead Horse Bay, located just inside the inlet mouth and a bit northeast at N40-35.082 W73-54.153, has accounted for good early season flounder action. Access to Dead Horse is easy, but small boaters definitely have the advantage.

Built in 1974, the Rockaway Artificial Reef became the first artificial reef in New York State waters. The reef is located about 4.2 nautical miles south/southeast of Rockaway Inlet, in 30 to 40 feet of water, at N40-32.500 W73-50.520. The reef was originally made up of large pyramids of tires, lashed together and filled with concrete. As time wore on, barge loads of clean concrete and steel from the demolition of the railroad bridge over the Reynolds Channel were added. To this day, the DEC continues to add rubble when a need arises. The area fishable is roughly 413 acres in size, so this is not your backyard pond—this baby has size to it.

For anglers, the reef is loaded with blackfish, sea bass, porgies, ling and bluefish. In addition, false albacore, bonito and weakfish roam the area in season. Fluke are often caught on the sandy fringes of the reef and at times on the reef proper by anglers dunking clam or squid baits for sea bass and porgies.

Since this reef is located in relatively shallow water—at least in comparison to wrecks or other reefs—it is also one of the first to come alive in the spring. In speaking with well-known writer and contributor to *The Fisherman* Magazine, Tony Salerno, I learned the following. "By early April, ling move into the shallow waters and dominate the reef until the waters begin to warm, and sea bass and blackfish move into the nooks and crannies. Anglers using clam strips, fish and crab bait on bottom rigs enjoy good action throughout the spring and early summer. If it's big fluke you're looking for, try drifting long strips of fluke belly on fluke rigs. From May through September, many fluke to 12 pounds are taken from the reef. Fork tail speedsters such as bonito and false albacore frequent the reef during the late summer and fall, as do the bluefish, with stripers always a possibility. Artificial lures such as Kastmasters, Hopkins, Crippled Herring and Deadly Dicks will all work. As the season swings into fall, porgies and sea bass dominate this reef with the blackfish joining forces by mid to late October. Clam and squid strips on hi-low rigs will work just fine on these species. As for blackfish, green and fiddler crabs, fished on Virginia number 5 tandem rigs, will keep you busy with the tog. Current is often not a factor along the Rockaway Reef; therefore, sinkers to five ounces will generally get the job done."

The reef is not far from the inlet, but anglers should be sure they are familiar with their craft, and the area's waters, before making the trek. Watch your weather and the tide and wind conditions, which could make the inlet a chore on the return trip. Should a storm or other inclement weather pop up, the run back to the inlet is relatively quick.

JAMAICA BAY

Having grown up on Long Island, and being the editor of *The Fisherman Magazine*, you would think I would have fished every body of water there is to fish locally. Well, you are pretty close to being right, but before writing this book, Jamaica Bay was one of those areas I had missed!

J-Bay is home to great striper action. Here's guide John McMurray with a fine 25-pounder.

HOT SPOTS

For this area, I went to a local expert—John McMurray of One More Cast. John not only fishes J-Bay more than anyone I know, he catches more too! We'll begin our J-Bay exploring on the east side of the bay.

Grass Hassock Bay, which is located just west of Inwood, on the east side of Jamaica Bay, can be easily accessed by boat from Beach Channel or one of the many marinas on the east side.

This bay, although small in comparison to Grassy, offers excellent action on school bass, cocktail and chopper blues. And, if the conditions are right, cow stripers of 30-plus pounds can be found cruising the shallows as well.

What makes Grass Hassock so lively is the abundance of creeks that feed the bay on the falling tide, compliments of the Jo Co Marsh. If you can combine a falling tide with daybreak, you're in perfect shape!

John likes to prowl the edges of these drains, casting small poppers, paddletail grubs, or the long wand with popping flies as the offering. Trolling motors are best as a stealth approach will usually not spook fish in the shallow waters, which range anywhere from one to two feet in close. There will be times when you can see dorsals of large bass or blues breaking the surface as they cruise, searching for an easy meal.

Moving into deeper water, the area near the Radar Pier has depths of 30-plus feet, and is a great area to chunk large bass or blues. If bunker are around, your best bet would be to snag one, and then live-line it for a larger bass.

After Grass Hassock, the next area on the east side is Grassy Bay. Traversing towards Grassy Bay, you'll pass the Silver Hole and begin to traverse north between East High Meadow Broad Creek Marsh, which will lead you right into Grassy Bay, and the train trestle area.

The first stop in this bay should be near the West Radar Pier, which offers several high and low points jumping around from 18, 12 and 30 feet. These humps and jumps should hold a fair amount of bait, which will offer good shots of bottom dwellers, as well as bass and blues.

Moving west in the bay, you'll begin to approach the "Trestle," an area well known for great striper action in the spring, summer and fall. According to John, this bay is rich with fish because the bunker never really vacate the bay, and are around all season long. Find the schools of bunker and catch a few for bait.

Another hot spot, especially for shorebound anglers, would be Canarsie Pier, located on the west side of J-Bay. The pier is easily located on most Hagstrom maps, and offers ample parking. Anglers dunking worms and clams have accounted for a few flounder, but most anglers will opt for the night tide, dunking bunker for blues or bass. In the fall, and early spring a good shot of herring arrive on the scene, with typical Christmas-tree type herring rigs producing bucketful of the tasty critters.

Moving south, the Cross Bay Bridge is a great spot for angling opportunities. The Cross Bay Bridge is the southernmost bridge connecting Howard Beach to the Rockaways, and spans Beach Channel.

According to Anthony Iannone of Cross Bay Bait and Tackle (164-26 Cross Bay Blvd., Howard Beach, NY), the spring flounder run is pretty good, but for larger fish, the fall is best. Blood and sandworms, with a heavy dose of chum, is the key. In the summer months, fluke and bluefish are the mainstays, especially fluke, with enough keeper size fish to make it worth the effort. As for blues, most are in the four- to eight-pound class, but some real brutes will show up when the bunker, a larger bait, shows in late July through August.

Over the last several years, the fall striped bass run has been phenomenal, and anglers feel it will only continue to get stronger with each year. In 2004, 20-pound bass were a common sight, with fish over 30 pounds showing as well. The best baits have been clams and bunker chunks. If I had to guess, I would bet my paycheck that a live kingfish, bergall, porgy or lafayette, would coax a brute from the abutment area on the dropping tide.

For shorebound anglers, access to Cross Bay Bridge is simple. Take any of the east/west thoroughfares on Long Island and head south. The bridge is the last one before you hit the Rockaways. From Brooklyn take the Belt Parkway to Flatbush Avenue and head south across the Marine Parkway Bridge (another hot spot) and backtrack east to the Cross Bay Bridge. For boaters, this is really just a Jamaica Bay option, via Runway Channel to Beach on the west side or through Grassy Bay and East Broad Channel from the east.

REYNOLDS CHANNEL

Reynolds Channel connects the inlets of Jones to the east with Debs (East Rockaway Inlet) to the west. The channel provides anglers the opportunity to catch virtually all of the aforementioned species, and can be home to true trophy catches.

Access to the channel is easy from any of the Long Beach Marinas, or by way of the mainland through Hempstead Bay or Middle Bay.

Easily identifiable on most charts, Reynolds Channel is home to hot spots such as the Lido Motel and Cement Block—great fluke spots with traditional spearing and squid baits; Railroad and AB (Atlantic Beach) bridges—solid striper haunts, and the Magnolia Pier. The pier is a much

Outdoor writer Tony Salerno took advantage of the super fluke action at Reynolds Channel and reeled in this 8-pounder.

better shorebound spot, but anglers drifting in front, on the outgoing tide, can catch keeper size fluke by day, and larger stripers after dark.

JONES INLET

For Jones Inlet, one of the best sources of information was Capt. Tom Mikoleski of the charter boat *Grand Slam*. Capt. Tom, along with his brother Capt. Pete of the "Miss Mac," have been fishing these waters for the better parts of their lives.

For access, Jones Inlet can be a treacherous one. Small boaters, or boaters not familiar with the area, should stay away from the inlet and wait until you can get seasoned local guidance. For skilled anglers, the inlet is quite fishable. Beginning in May, the West and east bars will produce striped bass on a regular basis. The West Bar will produce better, but they will both account for action. The key to fishing the bars is to anchor a safe distance away from the white water—usually you will be in 20 to 25 feet of water. The white water area can be as shallow as five to six feet, so stay clear of this area. Tom likes the outgoing tide, and fishes just west of the green can. Anglers can anchor up and drift clams to the white water or stem the tide utilizing the boat's motor, and then drift clams back. As for the East Bar, live eels fished in the fall work best.

Moving just inside Jones Inlet, anglers can pick away on flounder along the Short Beach Coast Guard Station area or Big Meadowbrook Bridge. The "Big M" is easy to find, as it is the first bridge east of the inlet proper. The bridge abutments will hold a good concentration of blackfish for shorebound fishermen and boaters alike. To fish for tog in this area, make sure the tide has slacked off. Fish one hour on each side as a guideline.

ZACHS BAY

According to Tony Salerno, an outdoor writer for *The Fisherman* Magazine, Zachs Bay is actually a deep-water cove, rather than a bay. The bay sees flowing water from Sloop Channel to the west and the State Boat Channel from the east. Despite the water in the channels flowing quite strong at times, the back of this bay is relatively current-free. Zachs Bay is easily traversed by boaters, but sees more recreational day-trippers than fishermen. The best times to fish this bay would be early in the season before the boating crowd gets going. Flounder will be the first choice, followed by cocktail blues and school stripers.

GREAT SOUTH BAY/FIRE ISLAND INLET

Great South Bay consists of an area roughly 24 miles long and 6 miles wide at its widest point, and is located between Bay Shore and Fire Island, just about in line with the Fire Island Lighthouse. The north side of the bay averages between three and 10 feet deep, with the deeper area reserved for the channels that dot the bay. The south side of the bay is slightly deeper overall, but is also made up of more channels, most of which are in the 15- to 20-foot depth ranges.

With the largest fleet of boats located on Captree Island in Babylon, anglers can hit the fishing grounds in comfort.

For anglers, the main portion of the bay that is fished is between the Babylon Cut, located northwest of Captree Island, and Patchogue on the north side. Moving south, the Fire Island Inlet area, back to Ocean Beach, is also fished heavily.

With a plethora of structure, channels and currents, plus sandy flats that hold bait, Great South Bay is an angler's delight. For boaters, there are two New York State Launch Ramps. The first is located on the south side of the bay at Captree State Park. This ramp offers anglers both day and night access, allowing easy access to the main portion of the bay, several deep channels, the State Channel, and the inlet proper. If you cannot connect with something in any of these areas, then you are not wetting a line! The second state ramp is located at Heckscher State Park on the north side of the bay. Here anglers can fish dawn to dusk. From Heckscher, prime weakfish and flounder hot spots can be found within minutes of launching your boat.

On the north side of the bay, virtually every town offers public ramps. These ramps however are mostly only open during daylight hours, and will garner a fee for out-of-town visitors.

A favorite hot spot for South Shore fans is the Copiague Hole. The Copiague Hole, located in the East-West Channel on the East Side of Tanner Park, is home to a plethora of species. The Copiague Hole is easily found by using your depth finder. The hole is at least 30-feet deep, with water of 8 to 10 feet surrounding it.

According to Bob Rose of Bob's Bait and Tackle in Amity Harbor, as the spring arrives, anglers working the area will be pleased by the winter flounder activity, and then with weaks throughout the summer. Although the weaks of the summer are generally in the keeper and smaller class, some fish of five to eight pounds are caught each year.

In the fall, anglers can expect to find a mix of bottom dwellers like sea bass, porgies, small weaks, kingfish and a few winter flounder. For striper fans, this close-to-home spot can offer quality action with live eels after dark.

The appeal of this area, besides being close to many home ports, is the depth. The hole is the deepest area of the bay, and was supposedly formed when houses on the mainland were built many years ago. It seems they needed fill, so the hole was dredged. The "Hole" is located east of Howells Creek off Howell Point in the East-West Channel. It is easily picked up on any bottom recorder or chart, as the depths drop from about 10 to 12 feet to 30 feet.

Angling opportunities are also available on one of the many party or charter boats that make up the Captree Fleet. With over a dozen boats to chose from, all sailing daily—sometimes twice and three times—you can always get a ride to the hot spot. The best feature of the party boats is that you need absolutely nothing in the way of tackle or gear. Just bring along appropriate clothing for the time of year, and within a short ride of the basin, you can be into non-stop action.

Fire Island Inlet offers anglers the opportunity to fish fast-moving ocean currents that flush the bay with "new" water each tide. This area is home to trophy stripers, fluke, chopper blues and weakfish. Try fishing the flats behind the Sore Thumb if you want super action with blowfish, winter flounder and kingfish.

Moving away from the inlet, and heading east, the first stop should be the Robert Moses Bridge. Here, anglers can catch school stripers on soft plastics, or dunk live baits and swimming plugs for trophies. Two years ago, James Harkins nailed a 50-plus pounder on a Rapala Shad Rap right under the bridge! The bridge also plays host to blackfish, mainly in the fall, which stage around the pilings picking away at crustaceans and such in the rubble.

The channels from the old wreck buoy and The Fisherman Reef area through to Atlantique is prime fluke grounds come June, while early May is prime time for tiderunner weakfish pushing the 10-plus pound mark. Several of the hot spots in this area are the Crazy Charlie buoy, Clam Pond and Kismet Reef. The reef is also a fine blackfish and sea bass hole in the fall.

Heading north in the bay you'll find West and Sexton islands. Two channels—Dickersons and West—split these, and offer solid angling opportunities. A little farther to the west, between Sexton and Captree Island, is another less traveled channel called Snake Hill that also produces well, especially winter flounder and weakfish. To access Snake Hill, anglers need to use a chart, or make sure they know the area. In speaking with Mike Andreani of Augie's Bait and Tackle, shallow bars and a width of no more than 100 feet at times will cause even the best helmsmen to run aground if not careful. Mike also said that any hard west or northwest wind, which dumps water out the bay, combined with low tide can make traversing Snake Hill difficult for even the most savvy angler.

As for fishing, flounder will show in the early spring, with fluke not far behind. As the summer progresses, weakfish and bay blues show in force. In tight along the beach side, school bass can be plugged in the early morning hours.

For tides, it is best to fish Snake Hill on the high turn. If you can combine this phase with an early morning or pea-soup-foggy day, when boat traffic is down, your catch ratio will quickly improve.

Snake Hill is a great place to fish, and a nice shortcut when coming south from Brightwaters, across to Captree and the State Channel. Just make sure you have a chart, as waiting for a tide or, worse yet, damaging your outboard will not help the day if you run aground!

Moving away from the boat scene, anglers can also enjoy catching their favorite species by fishing one of the many piers or jetties that dot the Great South Bay, especially on the north side of the bay.

Beginning to the west, Tanner Park, located in the town of Amity Harbor is easily accessible by way of Wilson Avenue, which is off Montauk Highway. In fact, Bob's shop should be your first stop, located on the left side! In speaking with Bob, Tanner Park Pier is similar to most on the South Shore in that it will see pretty good action from late April throughout the season. Flounder will be your first target, with fluke, blues, bass, kingfish, and all the crabs a family can eat!

Moving across the bay, towards the State Channel, Captree State Park is home to two very good piers. These piers, Fisherman's Wharf and Overlook, are accessed through the Captree State Park area. These piers are best known for their fluke and crab catches, but anglers can be rewarded with striped bass and blues on various tide stages. In fact, if you want large bass, fish the night shift on the dropping tide with some form of live bait.

In Babylon, the Babylon Town Dock is another good spot, especially for tiderunner weakfish and super crabbing as well. The Babylon Town Dock offers ample parking, and can be reached via car. Your best source of info for this area is Augies Bait and Tackle (631-669-9837) or Babylon Fishing Station (631-669-4503), both located just seconds from the dock at the end Fire Island Avenue.

There are three main docks from West Sayville to Patchogue—West Sayville Dock, Blue Point Dock and Patchogue's L-Dock. The first, West Sayville Dock is located in—obviously—West Sayville. This dock offers ample parking. Access to the dock is easy by way of Montauk Highway from any major roadway, to West Avenue in West Sayville. Take West Avenue south, and the dock is in front of you!

The dock will see some early season flounder action, however anglers have more fun with weakfish from early May throughout the summer. The dock also plays host to tons of blues, and in fact has seen keeper size striped bass caught as well.

Moving east to the Town of Blue Point, we'll find the Blue Point Dock. This dock is accessible by car by taking Blue Point Avenue, off Montauk Highway. According to Rick Torre, owner of Capt Ts Bait and Tackle, this dock sees flounder in the early season, while crabs, stripers, blues and snappers round out the season. For best action, the month of May is prime time.

The last of the docks in this string is Patchogue's L-Dock. This dock, which is open year round, holds a plethora of fish throughout our prime season—May through November. In speaking with John Mantione of J&J Bait and Tackle, May is again the best month, with good bluefish action, then fluke, snappers and crabs.

Moving to the pounding surf, Fire Island Inlet, and the surrounding sand beaches will produce quality action from spring through fall, with blues, bass and weaks the main quarry. The inlet proper is accessible by four-wheel drive truck—provided you have the right access permits—from April through December. Another four-wheel drive access point is the Sore Thumb, located off Ocean Parkway. For walk-on anglers, there are various parking fields available for after dark fishing as well.

In Fire Island Inlet, there are cuts and coves that trap baitfish on virtually every tide. These coves will be prime target areas for the surf angler—particularly on the dropping tide (current). Work small bucktails or lipped swimming plugs for best results. On the open beach, both sandworms or cut baits like bunker or herring are solid producers. In the fall, however, artificial lures will rule. I remember one fall day several years ago while fishing the Gilgo area, located just west of the Fire Island Inlet. Mullet had just begun filtering out of the bay, and big bass were hot on their tails. There were at least 10 buggies leap-frogging one another as we made our way west following the schools. Anglers were catching bass after bass, with fish to 35 pounds quite common. Then off in the distance I saw two trucks, bait rods out, catching nothing. As the fleet of buggies approached, and rods continued to bend with fish, the two guys never made an attempt to use an artificial. Well, we had fish on their left, and then jumped right past and continued catching. All the while the two bait rods went fishless! In the fall, when bait begins to move, use artificial lures!

FIRE ISLAND REEF

The Fire Island Reef, located outside Fire Island Inlet, approximately two nautical miles due south of the Lighthouse at N40-35.835 W73-12.480, is made up of varied debris, making for a great habitat for bottom-dwellers like porgies, sea bass and blackfish, not to mention the more predatory striped bass, bluefish and fluke roaming the outskirts.

The reef is made up of 1500 tires, laden with concrete, 10 barges, boat hulls, dry docks, armored tanks, coal waste blocks, concrete rubble and cesspool rings. And insiders believe that there are probably several other items on the reef as well, put there by private parties trying to "enhance" or isolate a specific region for their own purposes.

As summer approaches, the reef comes to life with porgies and sea bass making up the bulk of the action. With stripers still on the prowl in August, wire-line trolling accounts for a fair share of action as well. Blues can be busting the surface at any given time from then until the end of the fall run. As for fluke, try working just off the reef, with chrome balls tipped with squid and spearing, or tinker macs and whole squid.

Back to the bottom dwellers, porgies and sea bass. The key here is to locate the fish, use a little chum and keep them flying over the rails in what sometimes is non-stop action for hours.

Blackfish, although found during the summer, has a closed season, which could bode well for the fall fishery when it opens October 1. Green and fiddler crabs will work well, with clams and hermit crabs accounting for solid innings also.

For the private boater or party boat fleet, the Fire Island Reef is one of the hot spots all anglers can enjoy. At 744 acres, spanning 3,000 yards by 1200 yards, there is ample room for a fleet of boats.

MORICHES BAY/INLET

Moriches Inlet was formed by a Nor'easter in 1931, and then widened by the "Long Island Express" (the hurricane of '38). Moriches Inlet is considered "un-navigable at any time"—according to the Coast Guard—however countless anglers and boaters with local knowledge head through this inlet daily. Make sure, if you're venturing here, that you know what you are doing.

Probably one of the most sought hot spots is the Moriches Reef. This reef, which is made up of old tanks, concrete rubble, steel and a variety of other fish-holding structure, plays host to quality sea bass, porgy and blackfish action. In fact, anglers have also found doormat fluke on the reef in the summer months.

Moriches Inlet is accessible for the boating crowd via Moriches Bay, with launch ramps in Forge River, the Smith Point Bridge and Silly Lily Fishing Station. Anglers can also traverse the bay system from the west—Great South Bay, or east—Shinnecock Bay.

For the shorebound (surf) angler, the east side is accessible without four-wheel drive, but still requires a walk of over a mile. Access here is by way of Dune Road in Westhampton, and the Cupsogue County Park. For the angler to the west, the inlet is really only available to those holding a Suffolk County Four-Wheel Drive

The big red boat—*Rosie*—has been putting anglers into great fluke, flounder, porgy and sea bass action for many years.

access pass. With this, anglers can traverse the open beach for six miles, and wind up at the inlet. Keep in mind, however, that the beach may be impassable at times, causing a closure.

On the north side of the bay, there are two prominent fishing access areas for shorebound anglers. The first, Cranberry Dock, is located in the Narrows Bay area, near the Smith Point Bridge. This dock, which has ample parking, and room for about 10 to 15 anglers at a time, is a great early-season spot for flounder. As the season progresses, and May arrives, chopper blues and school bass will make up the brunt of the action.

The second spot is less fished, and is located deep inside Forge River. The Forge River Dock offers limited parking, but can offer good action for the kids in the way of snapper blues. Sharpies also cull a few decent weakfish from this pier in the early season. To reach Cranberry Dock, take Sunrise Highway to Exit 58, William Floyd Parkway. Head south on William Floyd about five miles to Havenwood Drive. Turn left and follow Havenwood to Cranberry Drive, and turn right. The dock is at the end of the road. For Forge River, get off at William Floyd Parkway heading south. Turn left onto Montauk Highway (Rte 27A), and go approximately three miles to Mastic Beach Road. Cross over the railroad tracks, and then make a left onto Patchogue Ave (the first left after the tracks.) As the road ends, bear right onto Riviera Drive and follow this to the dock, which will be at the end of the marina on your left.

The inlet proper is about 200 yards at its widest, with water depths pushing the 20 to 25 foot range. Strong currents make this inlet a tough one to navigate, especially on the dropping tide and a south wind. The inlet proper however is usually very accessible to fishing. The inlet is best known for the striped bass population, which sees fish in the 40-pound class, and larger, almost every year. Anglers score best when casting from the jetty with bucktails and eels or working live baits. Bluefish also roam the inlet from late May through November, eating everything in their paths. In the fall, blackfish will be along the rocks; most of these fish are on the small side, but dinner-size fish can be caught by shore or boat. The last of the predators available is fluke. Although in the flatfish family, fluke are extremely aggressive and will readily take live baits or bucktails adorned with long strip baits.

Moving outside the inlet, anglers can fish the Moriches Artificial Reef. This reef is located west and south of Moriches Inlet at N40-43.470 W72-46.485, approximately two and a half miles from the breakwater. The reef, which is called "Fish Haven" or "Moriches Offshore Reef," is clearly depicted on most charts. At 13 acres in size, the reef has ample room for all to enjoy. The reef is easily accessible to boaters leaving Moriches Inlet by way of the east or west cuts.

According to Chet Wilcox of B&B Tackle in Center Moriches, "The reef was originally started by the Moriches Anglers Club after receiving the appropriate permits from DEC. The first structure that was used was old tires filled with cement and small vessels. As time wore on, and DEC took control of permits for all reefs, the Moriches anglers took a back seat. When the DEC resumed supporting the reef in the way of Army surplus tanks, the club, along with other anglers and divers, rekindled their interest, and began thinking of how they could further improve the sight. Since that time, the Moriches Anglers have held various fund raisers ranging from golf tourneys to live auctions to help raise funds and continue building on this magnificent piece."

"As far as fishing is concerned," says Chet, "anglers can catch porgies, fluke, blackfish, sea bass, blues, stripers and even in occasional codfish!"

Staying outside the inlet, the next hot spot would be the Dredge Hole. The Dredge Hole came about due to the "Perfect Storm" of '92. The storm cut an opening in the barrier island called Pikes Inlet, which needed to be filled. The Dredge Hole resulted from sand dredged to fill Pikes Inlet.. The Hole is located outside Moriches Inlet, east of the Cupsogue Beach Pavilion, a few hundred yards offshore. This hole is home to bass, fluke, porgies, sea bass and bluefish.

At the Dredge Hole, anglers can expect fluke to arrive early, sometimes even before the season opens. Fluke will remain in the Hole most of the year, with larger fish always a possibility. In fact, Gary Grunseich of Silly Lily Fishing Station in east Moriches feels that the best time to target fluke is the fall, when the flatties begin to leave the bay. Gary's best, an 8 pounder, was caught here.

As for other bottom dwellers, porgies and sea bass, with an occasional blackfish, can be caught from late April through June, then again from September through November. Due to ever-changing rules regarding the opening and closing of seasons, be sure you are abreast of the season before targeting a specific fish. Early in the season, cocktail blues will be found near the Hole, and as summer approaches larger choppers will reside, readily taking jigs and chunks. As the fall moves closer, striped bass will hang around the Hole looking for an easy meal. These bass will readily succumb to live baits like legal size porgy, flounder, and bergalls, kingfish and layfayettes. A bergall is a small bait-stealing trash fish in the wrasse family. It has a small mouth and is found on wrecks and reefs, especially in areas where blackfish feed. Although a trash fish, it does have some angling value as a live-line bait; however, most anglers will do their best to avoid areas infested with these bait stealers. The layfayette is actually a spot (Leiostomus xanthurus). The spot is blueish gray above with golden reflections and silvery below, according to "Fishes of the Gulf of Maine" by Bigelow and Scroeder. Spot can get as large as 20 inches, but we rearly see fish more than 10 to 15 inches off Long Island. Spot will readily take worms and clams, and can be found around the same areas that fluke appear—sandy bottoms, mud or estuarine waters. Spot travel in schools, so if you catch one, there are sure to be plenty more lurking below.

In closing, keep in mind the Hole is about 60 to 70 feet deep, so a lot of lead may be needed to hold bottom. On calm, bluebird days, lighter tackle may suffice.

Heading north from the inlet, the first stops are the cuts—east and west. These cuts are heavily traversed in season, with anglers fishing on both sides. Fluke, stripers and blues are the mainstays. If you fish the dropping tide on the west side, and stay fairly close to the rocks, stripers will be found lurking. Live bait is the best way to go, with eels, bergalls, flounder and blackfish all accounting for action. Keep in mind that all live baits must meet the minimum New York State regulations. Another solid area is the flat located on the west and backside of the inlet. These flats see the water depth range from 20 feet to two feet!

Moving inside the inlet is Moriches Bay. Moriches Bay is centered between Bellport Bay to the west and the Quogue Canal on the eastern end. According to Gary Grunseich of Silly Lily Fishing Station, the bay is roughly five miles in long, which includes the Narrows area on the west. The average depth of this shallow bay is five feet deep, with several holes that go to 30 feet.

There are various coves, holes and flats, all of which are prime fish-holding areas. To the east is the "Hole," which is located at buoy 30/31, with another hole at 33, and an even deeper hole at 35. These holes will always offer super bottom fish action with layfayettes, porgies, triggerfish and sea bass the mainstays. In fact, if you live-line one of these species at slack water, you might stumble on a quality striper or chopper blue.

Moving back west, anglers can fish the Coast Guard Station, the mouth of the Forge River, the Narrows and Smith Point Bridge. The Forge River area is very muddy, but has a ton of baitfish, which can be found around every dock and well-lit pier. These areas are prime targets for weakfish in early May through June. Try using Fin-S Fish in pearl around lighted docks in the late evening hours. Sandworms will also account for action.

Closing out the action in Moriches are the buoy chains, which are great spots for triggerfish, blowfish, kingfish and porgies. Fish a squid or clam bait right at the buoy, and you'll be sure to bring home dinner. For anglers wishing to locate blackfish, the rock jetties, specifically the south end of the west side, will hold tog between two and six pounds on average.

QUANTUCK AND QUOGUE CANALS

The Quantuck and Quogue canals are the two small bodies of water that connect the eastern portion of Moriches Bay to the western portion of Shinnecock Bay. These canals, which in places are merely 50 feet wide, are one of the best early-season flounder hot spots on the South Shore. In fact, probably one of the best early-season spots on all of Long Island!

The canals are easily accessible through the town of Westhampton via Jessup Lane or Beach Lane. Upon arriving at the canals, there is limited parking, but enough to go around. The canals are best fished on the dropping tide, as water is flushed out of the feeder creeks, thus moving small bait into the waiting mouths of winter flounder.

The Shinnecock Canal is a favorite flounder hotspot, but also solidly produces fluke, weakfish, striped bass, and bluefish.

The canals also play host to a good supply of early-season bluefish, especially as bunker make their way from west to east through the canal and into Shinnecock Bay. This usually takes place in late May, and will last almost all summer. During this same period, striped bass will be caught as well.

SHINNECOCK BAY, INLET AND CANAL

For starters, the Shinnecock Canal is home to fantastic seasonal fishing for the shorebound angler. Located in Hampton Bays, the Shinnecock Canal is easily accessible to all, and allows night fishing as well. Ample parking is available, and there are two bait shops—Altenkirch Precision Outfitters and East End Bait and Tackle only minutes away. In fact, Altenkirch is right on the canal! All of the targeted species—blues, flounder, fluke, stripers, blackfish, weakfish, porgies and sea bass—can be caught at the canal during certain times of the year.

The Shinnecock Canal is the gateway between Shinnecock Bay and the Peconics. As the tides vary greatly in these areas, the canal is separated by a set of three locks, which close twice per day—and stay closed for a period of six hours each time. It is these times of closure and opening that makes for fantastic action. The locks open and close per the tides, closing 3½ hours before the high tide at Sandy Hook, and then opening 2½ hours after the high tide at Sandy Hook.

The best action at the canal is one hour before the locks close, throughout the closure period and then about a 45-minute window of opportunity after the locks open. Some anglers fish the canal area during peak open phases, but this is best left to the seasoned anglers as wicked currents and harsh bottom structure can sometimes frustrate the novice.

Access to the Shinnecock Canal is by way of Sunrise Highway. Take exit 66 and turn left at the bottom of the ramp on North Shore Highway (a small road). The road will end at Montauk Highway, where you will turn right, go over the canal, and then make your next right onto Newtown Road. Take this to the first right, Holzman Lane, and the canal is in front of you.

Next up on the Shinnecock list of hot spots is the Ponquogue Pier, located at the base of the new Ponquogue Bridge, located approximately one mile west of Shinnecock Inlet. The pier was not always a pier. In fact it used to be the only means of travel across Shinnecock Bay to the ocean. After years of storms battered the bridge, leaving it virtually useless as a crossover, the new bridge was constructed. The old bridge was separated at mid-span, leaving behind two productive fishing piers, in relatively close proximity to Shinnecock Inlet.

Alberto Knie fished the Shinnecock Canal (that's right, the canal!) for this pending IGFA World Record striper of 45.5 pounds, caught on 8-pound test line!

The south pier offers ample parking, and a boat launch for all to use. This pier is closer to the main channel, and offers slightly deeper water for anglers to work. With raging currents, the last hour of tidal movement is best, although large bass have been caught at mid-tide. In fact, I caught my largest bass, a fish of 40 pounds, from this bridge about six years ago. The current at the time was raging at 5 to 6 knots. I needed a 3-ounce bucktail to get anywhere near the bottom!

The north side is a longer pier, offering more room for anglers, but the parking is limited. This side sees better action with bottom fish, and bay blues as they corral small bait in the shallows. The end of the pier juts out enough however where anglers can reach the main channel, and work the faster currents and deeper water.

Blackfish are a main staple at the piers, but again, the fishing limited to the times of relatively slack water, or very slow-moving current. Divers have reported they have seen tog upwards of 15 pounds roaming the pier area; so make sure the tackle you use is stout!

Moving back into the bay proper, there are several really good areas for anglers to enjoy, and all are easily accessible by boat by way of any of the marinas that dot the shoreline. If you do not have your own boat, access is best by one of the local charter boats, or the party boat "Shinnecock Star," which sails daily in season.

According to resident sharpie and charter captain, Kevin Falvey (516-316-6688), "Anglers heading east will come to the area known as the Basket, which is located just north of the inlet proper. It produces good fluking once the fish move inside in July. Bass anglers also work the rips and small islands in this area, having good success on moving water, especially in September. West of the bridge, anglers will find great summer-long fluking along the bar that runs north to south at buoy 11. Fish the down-current side of the bar with traditional strip baits, 'ham n eggs' (spearing and squid), live killies or my favorite, live snappers in late August." Heading west of the bridge, anglers will come to Tiana Bay, a bay within Shinnecock Bay. Here, roving schools of blues, and good fluking will abound. Look for birds and bait to find the choppers and try fluking at Pine Neck Point. Best fishing here is on the flood, as this area of the bay gets very little tidal influence. As such late summer fishing here can be lackluster due to hot, non-oxygenated water. Another good spot is Ram Pasture, located between the Ponquogue Bridge and the bar at Buoy 11. The bottom off of Ram Pasture Point features sloughs and mussel beds. Anglers can expect good bass fishing, particularly while bucktailing during the top of the flood in May.

For anglers looking to get in on great action, the area outside Shinnecock Inlet is as sure a bet as you'll find. Whether it is fluke, sea bass, blackfish, bluefish or striped bass, this area has them all. Shinnecock Inlet is a relatively easy inlet to navigate, and is clearly marked. Follow through the inlet, and then pick your hot spot.

As for the inlet itself, it was formed during the same storm that widened Moriches Inlet—the "38 Express." This storm left hundreds dead in New England and wreaked havoc along the Long Island Coast. On the brighter side, the inlet has eased commercial travel of fishing boats, and created ample fishing opportunities for recreational anglers.

In speaking with Capt. Judy Schoerlin of the *Hey Jude* out of Molnar's Landing in Hampton Bays (631-728-1860), I found out that the ocean side of Shinnecock has been the hot area for fluke for several years now. In fact, several years ago, the first week of September saw 17 fluke over seven pounds weighed in, with the largest, a 14-pound, 10-ounce doormat weighed in by Mike Butler

For fluke fans, the area outside the inlet, to the east at the "Castle," is the hot spot. The "Castle" is located about ten minutes from the inlet, and is clearly identified by a large castle-like mansion, which is clearly visible. According to Judy, this area allows anglers deeper water, without having to travel miles offshore. Water depth ranges from 50 to 60 feet. Judy recommends large strip baits to up your chances at a true doormat of 8-plus pounds.

The ocean area is not just home to fluke. There are several structured areas that hold sea bass, blackfish and porgies. Heading straight out from the inlet, the Shinnecock Reef and sea buoy area will offer bottom fans a smorgasbord throughout the summer and into the fall. Anchor up, chum with clam or bunker, drop a baited hook with clam strips, crabs or squid, and you're sure to come home with dinner.

Blues are always roaming the area as well. In the late summer, the smaller cocktails can become a nuisance, but boy are they fun to catch. In fact, most anglers like the two to three-pounder for the barbecue.

As the fall approaches, striped bass will begin setting up shop. They will stage in the inlet, but can be found along the open beaches as soon as larger bait, like herring, bunker or snapper blues, are in the ocean. Watch for the first cold snap, which is usually in line with a nor'easter, for great action.

Before leaving the Shinnecock area, you have to stop at Tulley's Seafood Market for a hot bowl of clam chowder. In fact, their fish, clams, and seafood are so good that if I come home empty when my wife knows I fished there, I am ordered to return for the "goods!" Tim, the owner, prides himself on the freshest available seafood around, and in fact works with several local commercial anglers for top-shelf seafood at all times.

MECOX AND SAG PONDS

Although the ponds, which are both located in Southampton, do not offer fishing opportunities per se, they do offer great action for surfcasters and boaters alike when they are opened to the ocean. Both ponds are rich with juvenile baitfish and crabs, plus an ample supple of alewives. Mecox is the larger of the two.

The ponds are usually opened manually in the spring, and then again in the fall. The real problem here is knowing when they have been opened. Although it is usually a word-of-mouth proposition, the local fishermen have a good handle on the openings. Another great source is Ken Morse at Tight Lines Tackle (631-725-0740) in Sag Harbor. Kenny pretty much knows when they open, and will be happy to disseminate the info.

After the ponds open, and the bait begins to flush into the open Atlantic, predators in the form of cow bass of 30-plus pounds and chopper blues will make their way to the cuts. Both surf anglers and boaters alike can cash in on this action. For boaters the key is to stay

Steve Pluchino duped this 47-pound striper while fishing a pencil popper at the Ponds.

off the beach and cast towards the outflow. A word to the wise is to be courteous to surfcasters as well. Do not cast into their lines, simply move down the beach a bit.

For casters on shore, daylight action is best with metal-lip swimmers, poppers and bucktails, while after dark, live eels and six-inch Bombers in the jointed style work best.

Access to the ponds by boat can be made from Shinnecock Inlet. Mecox is about six miles east, while Sag is another two to three miles east of Mecox. For the surf crowd, Sag and Mecox can be walked to from the local town parking lot, or you can gain beach access with a Southampton Town Sticker ($200 for non-residents).

To access Mecox without the town pass, simply take Rte 27, Sunrise Highway east to Mecox Road. Head south (right turn) on Mecox and follow it to Jobs Lane. Stay on Jobs until it ends and go left onto Dune Road. Take this to the parking lot and park. Although this is a town lot, parking restrictions are lax in the fall.

As for Sagaponack (Sag Pond), take Sunrise Highway a little farther east to Sag/Main Road, which is just east of Bridgehampton. Follow the road until it ends and park. For both areas, a short walk across the dunes, and then to the beach will put you at the pond's entrance to the ocean.

MONTAUK POINT

We'll just give you some tidbits on famed Montauk Point here—but devote an entire chapter to it later on. See this chapter for a detailed discussion.

For anglers wanting to fish Montauk, besides surfcasting, the only way is through Montauk Harbor. Whether you use your own boat, or board the many party or charter boats, the harbor is the way out to the fishing grounds.

Montauk Point is probably one of the most famous areas for fishing along the East Coast. Anglers will come from as far away as California to fish "Mecca." Montauk, with virtually every species found on Long Island available, also offers anglers the ability to fish various tides and remove themselves from certain wind patterns not conducive to having fun. At Montauk, if the wind is howling out of the north, anglers can work the South Side. This especially comes into play in the early stages of the season when fluke are the mainstay. Areas like Gurneys and the Radar Tower are all fluke magnets. If the wind is honking in a southerly fashion, the Shagwong Reef is a hot spot for stripers, fluke and bluefish.

One area that always plays host to a plethora of boats is the Elbow. The Elbow is located slightly northeast of the famed

Most anglers may not land a bass like Jimmy George's 69.15-pounder, but fish over 40 pounds are a pretty common sight at Mecca.

Lighthouse and runs in a northeast direction toward Block Island. The Elbow is home to some of the best striper action an angler can ask for. Year after year, "cow" stripers over 40 pounds are recorded. The best catches by day are had with wire line, while trolling parachute jigs. Parachutes in green, tipped with pork rind, are striper killers. Another proven method is trolling bunker spoons, especially off the south side, near the Great Eastern area. In fact, two years ago, Jimmy George boated a 69.15-pound striper on a homemade bunker spoon. This was the largest bass caught off Long

Island in some time—despite several 50-plus-pound fish recorded each year.

Although Block Island is located in Rhode Island waters, this hot spot is easily reached by any seaworthy craft leaving Montauk Harbor. At roughly a 12-mile ride, Block offers a plethora of action. In the fall months, anglers will be pleased with sea bass and porgies, with chopper blues and large stripers in the mix. For the smaller porgies and sea bass, dropping baits to the bottom is your best choice. For the blues, watch for birds diving on bait, and then chase down the schools and throw topwater plugs. For cow stripers, nothing beats a live eel after dark fished close to the rocky shoreline.

Moving back towards the harbor, Lake Montauk is home to super flounder action in the early stages of the year, and then sees a good fluke bite as the summer unfolds. In between the fluke and flounder, cocktail blues will usually raid the lake as well. Although called Lake Montauk, this is a saltwater body of water, with chang-

While on Capt. Bob Rocchetta's *Rainbow*, Russ Drake boated this 58.6-pounder on a live eel.

ing tides and currents. There is also a rental station—Uihlein's, right on the lake—which rents boats for an anglers' pleasure. In fact, the boats are not just for the lake as vessels in the 30-foot class are available as well.

Other hot spots around Montauk include Washington Shoal, located just off Shagwong. This shoal plays host to a great fluke bite throughout the months of June and August, and will see ample action with stripers and blues, not to mention the albie and bonito action in the fall.

Moving farther north from Washington Shoal in a northwest direction, anglers will come to the Cerberus Shoal area, located at N41-10.24 W71-57.16. This shoal, according to Capt. Bob Rocchetta of the "Rainbow," is covered in lobster pots, which makes fishing difficult at times. However, porgies will be abundant at this spot all summer long, while blackfish will be the mainstays come fall. For trollers, bass and blues can be trolled up in the rips. Anglers should head to Cerberus with caution as this is wide-open water, subject to rough seas on almost any wind direction. Adding into the equation are the many large ships that pass near the Shoal on their way into Long Island Sound.

GARDINERS ISLAND AREA

Southwest of Gardiners Island is an area known as Cherry Harbor. Although not a harbor *per se*, this area offers anglers some of the most beautiful scenery off Long Island. With Gardiners Island as a backdrop, combined with pristine clear water, the trip will be worth the time and effort even if you do not catch fish. Anglers heading west from Montauk Harbor or out of Sag Harbor will find the entire Gardiners area within easy reach.

As for fishing, in the early portion of the year—late April into May—fluke will be found in the area. Farther south, off Lionhead, located southwest of Cherry Harbor, anglers will be rewarded with super porgy action along this rocky shoreline. This area is often protected from southwest winds, making for a small tin boat, kayak or fly caster's dream. School blues and bass will often raid the area in the early morning hours. In fact, anglers can actually sight cast, similar to Florida flats action, for bass and marauding bluefish.

Moving to the east from Lionhead, the entire area near Cartwright Island, located N41-00.000 W71-48.500, is another fly caster's hot spot. The shallow water surrounding this island, all the way up to Gardiners proper, will see solid morning or dusk action for light tackle or fly casters. Most of the fish will be in the school class, 10 to 15 pounds at best, but tons of fun.

Heading back north, and to the east of Gardiners, anglers will find the famed Tobaccolot Bay, which was once home to some of the finest flounder action an angler could want. Recently however, the best action would be on fluke, with the edges of the area your best spots. Just north of Tobaccolot is Eastern Plains Point, which is a porgy and sea bass Mecca.

The north end of Gardiners, with all its rips and contours, will offer ample action on fluke, stripers and blues. The fall however is the time when larger bass in the 30-plus pound class can be found by anglers dunking live baits at dusk, or live eels after dark.

Moving a bit north of Gardiners is the "Ruins," located at N41-08.50 W72-08.77. The Ruins is quite attractive, and offers a bit of history for anglers and pleasure boaters alike. As for fishing, the area will almost always hold an ample supply of sand sharks up to six feet in length—a sure child pleaser! These harmless sharks will be caught on bunker chunks meant for stripers. When hooked, they always fool the angler into thinking they have hooked Moby bass. The area is also home to good fluke action when other surrounding areas seem to be devoid of life. The cooler waters seem to hold bait, and in turn keep the fluke biting throughout the dog days of summer. In the fall, green bonito and false albacore will have fly anglers running and gunning for the little speedsters, with fly rod in hand.

On the North Fork of Long Island, there is a chain of islands—Plum, Great Gull, Little Gull and Fishers—that offer anglers the opportunity to fish some of the wildest waters on the East Coast. Although these waters hold fish, a word of caution is advised. According to Capt. Bob Rocchetta of the *Rainbow* out of Orient, "You had better have knowledge of this area as one slip up could make you part of the reef system!" Bob suggests that you either familiarize yourself beforehand, or take one the many charter boats in the area. Another good source of info would be A.P. White's Tackle or WeGo Fishing Bait and Tackle.

The island chain provides the angler with four hotspots, which are tops on most skippers' lists. They consist of Plum Gut, Sluiceway, Race and Fishers Island Sound. The reefs in this area provide anglers with the greatest opportunity for action in our area. Your best shot at a cow bass—35 pounds or larger—is after dark. Anglers using live eels have scored with many a 50, and even some larger the last several years.

Another option for anglers would be to fish the early morning hours, staying close to the islands' rocky shorelines. These shorelines will provide super sight casting opportunities for the fly or light tackle angler.

As we head north of Orient Point, the Narrows area, located between the Connecticut River and Orient Point, is loaded with deep-water action and fast currents. Blackfish action is best in the fall, with any of the boulder-strewn areas a good starting point. For anglers looking to troll the area, blues can be caught all summer long. As summer rolls in, fluke in the six pound range will be caught using larger baits, drifted close to the bottom.

Closing out the North Fork area would be a quick ride across the Sound to Connecticut and the Connecticut River. Although covered in depth in Bob Sampson's *Fishing the Connecticut and Rhode Island Coasts*, here's a quick glimpse at what anglers can expect. The area plays host to bass throughout the year, but in the fall, the foliage, clear water, and dusk combine to make for one of the most rewarding days you'll have on the water.

GREAT PECONIC BAY

For the Great Peconic Bay area, the best source in my mind was resident sharpie and tackle shop owner Ken Morse. Ken has owned Tight Lines Tackle for over 20 years, and has fished the area for the better part of his life.

Beginning way up inside the Peconic Bay area are feeder creeks that begin to produce small baitfish in the early spring. These creeks are the beginning of the food chain for the entire year. Anglers would be wise to start at Red Creek, Bullhead Bay or Cold Spring Pond. All three of these offer easy access, plus an ample supply of baitfish. For early season action, school stripers will begin showing as early as March, with a better influx from mid-April throughout May. On the outgoing tide, the various baitfish will drop out of the creeks. Anglers either working the shoreline or from a boat can cash in by using small spoons, bucktails or Fin-S Fish soft plastics. For the shorebound angler, Towd Point—directly south of Nassau Point—and inside the Flanders Bay area are good starting points.

As warmer waters of spring arrive, blackfish can be caught at Rogers Rock. Rogers Rock is located just west of Robins Island at N40-57.34 W72-28.27. Your best chance of action will be on the last of the flood tide, and using soft baits like clams and worms. Although anglers love crabs, in the early season, the soft baits seem to produce better. Depending on the seasonal closures, porgy action is also very good at Rogers Rock. Use small pieces of clam and a chum pot, and you'll be sure to score.

Come late April and throughout May, weakfish action really begins to heat up. For Peconic Bay anglers, any of the drop-offs near Jessup, Nassau Point and Robins Island, plus the deep holes—like Sharks Hole, or the ones off Jessup in the Buoy 16 area—are all good producers. Weakfish, usually in the two to five-pound class can be tough fighters, and put up a battle for light-tackle fans. But be prepared as anglers have battled yellowfins upward of 15-plus pounds, and believe me, these babies are still around. In fact, each

HOT SPOTS

Dr. Paul "Sharp Hook" caught this 8.9-pound tog while with Capt. Jim House on the *Coyote* out of Orient. *Photo courtesy of Tony Salerno.*

year we see more and more 10-plus pound fish hitting the local tackle shop scales.

Striped bass season officially opens in New York State on April 15th, but it isn't until mid-May that bass in the 20-plus pound class begin showing up. For anglers seeking larger bass in this class, one of the better starting points would be the east side of Robins Island. There you will find large rocks where bass can hide and wait on an easy meal getting flushed by with the tidal current. Live eels, large legal-size swim baits, plus trolling wire have all accounted for solid action.

Another solid producer of stripers is Paradise Point, located opposite of the west side of Shelter Island on Great Hog Neck. At Paradise, your best action will be had jigging diamonds. In fact, some anglers even throw on a teaser hook about 20 to 30 inches above the Diamond Jig. Tip this hook with a sandworm, and you might grab a tiderunner weakfish. The main feature of this area is the swift moving currents that funnel through. The narrow area is a bait magnet, with predators looking for an easy meal.

The Sag Harbor Ferry Slip has been known to hold bass as well. Fishing is not actually inside the slip, but rather in the deep-water channel in front of it. By trolling the western hump of this area with parachute jigs, large tubes, or metal lips, or by dragging large tubes and sandworms, anglers have scored with fish well over 40 pounds. And it's all within easy reach for trailer boaters and the charter boat operators.

One of the most sought after fish on Long Island is the fluke or summer flounder. The fluke is fished harder by more anglers than any other species. The Peconics has always been known for quality fluke action, with best results in early May through June, when large fluke follow the squid into the area. The fluke encountered in this time could easily push the 10-pound mark, and in fact, fish in the high teens have been recorded as recently as 2004!

According to Ken, the most prominent spot would be the Greenlawns area, to Hay Point, and then onto Jennings. This area, which is located on the west and north side of Shelter Island, offers deep water—60-plus feet in some spots—and a fairly fast moving current—great for squid. The key to scoring here is big baits. Anglers using typical spearing and squid baits score well, but for the really big fluke, try using 10 to 12-inch bluefish fillets, whole squid, or bunker fillets. You may not get a lot of bites, but you can bet your bottom dollar that when the tug comes, the fluke will be of the doormat size.

Staying with fluke action, the Bug Light area is a classic transition area where waters go from 15 to 20 feet down to 50 to 60 feet in just a couple of hundred feet! The area is super for summer flatties on the outgoing tide. Try using heavy lead balls tipped with large fillets from bluefish or whole squid.

Moving closer to the town of Sag Harbor, the Sag Harbor Cove, which is located south of town under the stationary Sag Harbor Bridge, offers great worm hatches in the early spring. This area is prime for small boat and shorebound anglers. Canoes, kayaks, tin boats and wading will all produce well, especially for fly casters. For shorebound anglers, working bucktails, small swimming plugs like Bombers or Yo-Zuri hard plastics, and live eels after dark could yield large stripers in the 25 to 30-pound range. Fish the dropping tide for best results.

SHOREHAM PIPELINE

The Shoreham Pipeline is located just west of Wading River Creek, approximately one mile off the Shoreham Jetty. "The Pipe" can be detected as an approximate 10-foot rise off the bottom. Once you have located it, any area along its length will hold fish.

Anglers can access the Pipe via Mt. Sinai or Port Jefferson harbors. In speaking with a buddy of mine, Bob Danielson, who fishes the area with regularity, the Pipeline is a quick 15-minute hop from Port Jefferson.

Anglers can anticipate solid blackfish action here from early April, right through the winter months. Be aware, however, that seasonal closures do not allow you to target blackfish from June 1 to September 30. Although the spring bite is good, the fall is the better time to be on the Pipe. Green crabs, hermits and fiddlers, along with clams, have proved best in the bait department. With an abundance of life forms attaching and living near the Pipe, it is the prime habitat for big blackfish. In fact, several fish over 10 pounds will be caught each season.

The water depth is in the 25 to 30-foot range. Plan on stout tackle in the 20 to 25-pound class, matched to a good revolving spool reel like a Shimano Tekota or Penn 975. Some anglers prefer mono, but I like to go with a braid—Power Pro, Berkley Fireline or a similar line. The braid allows you to feel the lightest of blackfish taps, and it aids in quickly getting the black's head turned and away from any structure.

The Pipe has a tendency to steal rigs. Come prepared with a mess, as lost rigs will be commonplace on the Pipe. You can save a few by tying in an overhand knot to your sinker dropper, or by using lighter line on the three-way swivel to the sinker. This way when the sinker becomes lodged, the lighter line will break, losing only the sinker and not the entire terminal rig.

Known for blackfish, the Pipe will offer good summer action for bottom bouncers as well. In the last several years, the porgy action has been non-stop on both tides, with some anglers complaining they cannot get past the feisty scup to target the sea bass found in the area as well. Closing out the action at the Pipe will be stripers, blues and the little Atlantic speedsters—bonito and false albies.

Stripers can be caught by livelining legal-size porgies. Blues will be found crashing the surface, with artificial lures or tins your best bet. As for the speedsters, the fly rod and a Clouser fly are best.

MT. SINAI HARBOR

Mt. Sinai Harbor is located on the North Shore, just east of Port Jeff. Although it may not be one the prime stopping points on most angler's minds, there is enough action to make a trek inside worth your while.

In the early stages of the year, from April to May, flounder action is good near the docks and mouth of the inlet. As the months pass, fluke begin to be caught at the mouth, while bass and blues show inside the harbor.

By late May, bass, blues, fluke and even a few weakfish will make up the brunt of the catches. In fact, if you arrive at the backside of the harbor in the early morning hours, chopper blues in the teen-size class can be found raiding schools of bunker. The best time is daybreak and a dropping tide. Use topwater poppers and hold on.

Blues roam the waters of the Sound from mid-May throughout October. Both shorebound anglers and boaters sure have a blast! *Photo courtesy of Eric Burnley.*

For striper fans, early morning combined with high tides is best along the back marsh lines. As for blues, watch for bait breaking the surface on the dropping tide and either cast a popping plug, or drop a fresh bunker or herring chunk over the side.

Fluke fans will find the best action near the mouth on the dropping tide as bait flushes out of the harbor. A typical fluke rig tipped with spearing and squid will work fine. I prefer the west side, opposite the dock. The dock gets a lot of pressure, so I feel more fish will congregate on the opposite side. The opposite side also sees far less boat traffic as it is slightly shallower.

Another good spot is the pier area near the mouth of the harbor. Although not as plentiful as in years past, blackfish have been known to take green crabs worked against the pilings. If you use green crabs here, split them if they are small, and quarter them if they are large. The blackfish here are not jumbos, so a smaller portion will work best.

The harbor hosts a myriad of baitfish for predators to feed on. At times, I have even heard of a stray albie or bonito, but most times they stay just outside. For the fly rod enthusiast, the harbor will offer ample protection from the elements, plus a place to cash in on school bass, chopper blues and weakfish. In fact, the occasional fluke can be caught with a Clouser fly-fished close to the bottom.

It may not be one of the larger harbors on Long Island, but Mt. Sinai is definitely worth a look.

PORT JEFFERSON HARBOR

One of the largest harbors, if not the largest on the North Shore, Port Jeff Harbor is well protected from wind from virtually any direction. The harbor, which plays home to Caraftis Fishing Station, offers anglers a chance to catch striped bass, bluefish, porgies, snappers and more. Caraftis' offers rental boats, plus there is a town ramp for trailer boaters. The harbor also is home to the Port Jeff-to-Connecticut ferry service, so watch out for these cruisers. Access to Port Jeff Harbor is simple by following Route 112 north from any major east/west highway on Long Island until it ends. The harbor will be right in front of you!

For porgy anglers, the areas in deeper water near the buoys are best, but anglers working just outside the mouth, near Oldfield Point, will also cash in on great action. Try using worms or clams for best results. For novice fans, use your electronics to find any hump or bottom obstruction. For real sharpies, use your electronics to locate schools of porgies hiding near underwater rocks, ledges or small reefs.

If you like bluefish, then this is the harbor for you. This harbor is similar to most on the North Shore in that blues will raid the harbor virtually every day from late May through September, chasing schools of baitfish. Large fish in the teen class will be found in August chasing adult bunker. Most anglers will use dead bunker chunks, but I have found that fresh bunker, especially the heart section, will produce better. Livelining bunker will account for larger blues and big stripers.

Striped bass action can produce some large fish—20 plus pounds—but most of your action will be on teen-size fish and smaller. Work plugs along any of the banks in the early morning, and you're almost guaranteed success. The banks are loaded with grass lines. If you can pick a grass line that is just below the surface, try ripping a small Bill Lewis Rattle Trap across the tip tops. Bass will come charging at this offering.

Moving to the shallower parts of the harbor and Conscience Bay, anglers can find good flounder action from late May through June. Anglers can come with a limit, or at least enough for a healthy dinner by dunking worms, clams and mussels, combined with a heavy dose of clam chum.

CONSCIENCE BAY

Located just northwest of Port Jefferson Harbor is Conscience Bay. This bay, although rather small, offers anglers great action on with blues and stripers. The majority of action will be found in the fall, as baitfish begin to migrate out, making an easy target for larger predators. The soft mud bottom filled with bivalves and tiny crustaceans makes this bay a flounder-pounders hotspot. In fact, according to my buddy and fellow outdoor writer Tony Salerno, "The month of April and then again in November produces some of the finest quality size flatties in the area. Although the quantity of flounder is nowhere near the numbers of a decade ago, anglers who put in the effort during the spring and fall are usually rewarded with enough for dinner."

PORPOISE CHANNEL

Porpoise Channel is actually the channel that allows anglers' access to Stony Brook Harbor. Located on the southeast side of Smithtown Bay, this channel funnels baitfish in and out on virtually every tide. According to Fred Roth of Ronkonkoma Outfitters, the drawback with Porpoise is access. Boaters must traverse the Sound via Port Jefferson Harbor to the east or by way of Huntington Harbor to the west, both of which are a decent haul. Hopefully in the coming years, the new state-owned facility in Kings Park will offer a public ramp, which will give all anglers easy access.

What makes Porpoise a viable option for anglers is that the area is loaded with grass lines, which hold baitfish of all types, forming a mini-nursery. This mini nursery allows bait to grow and flourish, and then become dinner!

Anglers working deep inside Stony Brook Harbor will find decent flounder action in the early spring, with stripers, blues and fluke available from May through the fall The winter action here is somewhat quiet.

According to Fred, "If I were to pick the best-case scenario, it would be the grass lines along the mini-channel that runs near Stony Brook Yacht Club. This area must be fished at high tide, and then the first hour or two of the drop due to it's being relatively shallow. At low water, you cannot fish the area at all. Another hot spot, especially in late June and July, is the Stony Brook dock area, where large blues can be found in the early morning chasing bunker pods."

NISSEQUOGUE RIVER

The Nissequogue River, located on the North Shore in Smithtown, is home to super angling opportunities for freshwater fans, saltwater boaters and the surf crowd. Throughout the winter months, trout anglers will use small spinners and worms for sea run browns, some pushing the 10-plus pound mark. The river is easily accessible via 25A, and is clearly marked on any road map (Hagstrom Suffolk County is best).

Beginning at Caleb Smith State Park, trout fans can enjoy some of the best action on the island. As we move north from the park, Whites Pool, located just south of "The Bull" in Smithtown has been a hot spot for winter and summer trout for as long as I can remember. In fact, my mom used to allow me to skip school to fish opening day! I remember one opening day when I was young. The weather was cool, and the tide, unbeknownst to me, was low. I waded to Whites Pool in my hip waders, fished all morning, and then made the trek towards the parking lot. I was scared to death as the water was a lot higher, and I thought I was going to drown. After realizing there was no safe way, without swamping my hip boots, I just ran as fast as I could, hoping I would not fall. I was totally soaked when I arrived at the parking lot. Anglers should beware of the tidal waters. Although you are freshwater fishing, the tide rises and falls in brackish water areas like this one.

Continuing north on the river, anglers enjoy super action on sea run browns. According to John Richy of Terminal Tackle in Smithtown, the best bet for these bruisers is nightcrawlers or trout worms. Live killies are a good bait as well, but tough to get in the winter months when the browns are active.

As we get closer to spring, early season action on flounder and stripers make up the bulk of the excitement, with blues and even albies filtering in and out as the summer continues. Striper action in the spring can be fabulous as schools of sand eels make their way out of the river. Use small tins or swimming plugs after dark and you're sure to catch a few. The dock at the end of Dock Road is as good a starting point as you'll find.

Fluke will show during a typical year right after Memorial Day, with the best area between the mouth and the first bend, just before the yacht clubs. Small bucktails, squid and spearing combos will work well, as will killies.

As the fall approaches, stripers will make up the bulk of the catch, with bass hanging around until after Thanksgiving. If you're looking for a larger striper, however, October is the month. Large bass over 30 pounds can be caught on live eels and sandworms. "Don't overlook artificials either, as one of the largest bass I can remember, a 51 or 52 pounder, was caught on a five-inch Rebel several years ago," stated John.

For the surf crowd, the mouth of the river will see runs of chopper blues in the fall, with bass from school size to the big boys in the fall. Weakfish action, although they have comeback, is still a little on the slow side.

SMITHTOWN BAY

Smithtown Bay, located in between Eatons Neck and Crane Neck, is a large area, with troughs of water that run the shoreline. "In fact, this area is as close to Florida flats fishing as you'll get on Long Island," said Fred. Fred also observes that Smithtown Bay is similar to a wash basin—checking a map of the area, you will see how bait and predators will follow the currents in towards shore from Eatons of Crane, depending on the tide, and then circle back around as they come to either tip. Fred notes that this wash-basin effect keeps the predators in the area for tide after tide, and never allows the baitfish to run the beach.

Smithtown Bay is also somewhat sheltered from weather. Unless the wind is really cranking out of the north, most wind conditions will allow anglers to fish the shoreline out to the artificial reef and beyond.

Moving away from Smithtown Bay, but in close proximity, is the area just outside Flax Pond. Flax Pond is located just east of Crane Neck, mid-way to Oldfield Point. With moving water on the dropping tide, large fluke have been taken close to shore here each year. For porgy anglers, there is enough structure to hold good-sized scup in the spring and fall seasons. Remember, when targeting porgy or any other saltwater fish, to check out the size, number, and seasonal regulations with DEC or a local tackle shop to ensure you are within proper legal boundaries.

SMITHTOWN ARTIFICIAL REEF

The Smithtown Artificial Reef is actually located within the Smithtown Bay confines at N40-55.57/W73-11.04. The reef is roughly three acres in size and is mainly made up of barges, tires, and concrete-filled steel cylinders. The water depth is between 36 and 40 feet deep. Similar to most artificial reefs, this one was built to accommodate anglers and divers.

In the early part of the season, anglers can anticipate good action with blackfish, porgies and sea bass, all of which will show up looking for an easy meal. Clam, squid or worm-baited bottom rigs will all account for action. For larger species like bass and chopper blues, live-lining legal-size porgies, sea bass, or blackfish will work best.

As the waters cool in the fall, blackfish will be your best bet. Assorted fish will begin to migrate to the area, feeding heavily on the abundance of barnacles and crustaceans available within the area's structure. Similar to Mt. Sinai, you may not find a lot of large blackfish here. So, when choosing your bait, use fiddler crabs, or make sure to quarter or halve your green crabs. In the spring, sand worms will also work well.

The reef is not hard to fish, but anglers must pay attention to the tides and know exactly where you are fishing. By using a good quality fishfinder, you will be able to locate bottom profile, plus schools of fish. The last of the flood and most of the ebbing tide is best, as the current at mid-tide tends to be quite strong which makes anchoring and fishing difficult, but not impossible.

Anglers should avoid days when there is a stiff breeze out of the east or west. Fishing conditions on the reef can be tough on such days, and usually it will mean a tough day of catching as well.

HUNTINGTON BAY

Located on the North Shore, between Eatons Neck and Lloyd Neck, Huntington Bay is home to some of the finest fluke action the island has to offer. According to George Valentine, owner of Four Winds Bait and Tackle in Huntington Station, "Fluke action will get started as early as May, and continue right through the close of the season." George also said that as the fall approaches, many anglers abandon fluke for bass and blues—something he and Cor (George's wife) won't do, as they just love fluke fishing!

In late May or early June the hottest area is probably just outside Huntington Bay from the Brushpile to Ashroken Beach, with fish from four to six pounds quite common.

The area from the Coast Guard Station—located on the tip of Eatons Neck—and south to West Beach, then around to Sand City, will produce until the end of July.

As the water warms, you'll need to move off the beach to deeper water in the 30-foot range where the water is cooler. In fact, larger fish in the five to six-plus-pound class will show at the Triangle by July in the 60 to 70-foot depths.

According to George, "Most of my guys use Spro bucktails tipped with black shad. These work very well early, while white takes over as the summer approaches. For me, I always use a hi/lo rig. The lower hook will be a bucktail, while the teaser will be located 18 inches above, and six to eight inches off the standing line."

For bait the typical spearing and squid combo work well, but George likes to use a single bait on the bucktail, and a combo on the teaser hook. Some anglers prefer a combo bait on both. In the shallows, one-ounce bucktails will suffice, especially if you're using a braid. For the deeper water areas, adjust the weight as needed to get to the bottom.

In a normal season, you won't have to go deep for fluke as the rocky shore near Target Rock and the Old Centerport Channel offer nasty bottoms that fluke just love. Fluke don't always just lie in the sand; they are as aggressive as any predator fish.

As the fall approaches, the deep-water areas will see keepers in the bay, especially when snappers are prevalent. By the time fall rolls in, however, the blue and bass scene takes over, with choppers and cows making their way into the area.

For blues, jigging works best, while stripers will readily take chunk baits, live snappers, kingfish, eels and other baits.

MATINECOCK POINT

Located outside Hempstead Harbor, approximately ½-mile to the east, Matinecock is probably one of the best spots for weakfish in the Sound. This area, beginning with the full moon in June, will see solid action on weaks. And, these are not summer run weaks,

When fishing the Huntington area, make sure to bring a big cooler.

but large eight to 12-pound class fish, willing to take soft plastics or live baits.

Matinecock is also a small boat area—great for tin boats or craft under 18 feet with shallow drafts. The area is loaded with rocks, some touching the surface, even at high tide. A prime manta shrimp locale, the weaks will come in droves to feed on these crustaceans. Keep in mind that the bite is somewhat short-lived, sometimes only lasting three to four weeks or less.

HEMPSTEAD HARBOR

Moving inside Hempstead Harbor, the area south of the power plant, near Bar Beach, is the most productive early-season spot for winter flounder. And, although you will see good striper action in the channels, flounder pounders will feast on this area from opening day throughout the spring.

Capt. Rich Tenreiro of R&G Charters attempts to remove the hooks from this feisty blue.

For shorebound anglers, Hempstead also offers good access, but sometimes parking is limited. However the imaginative angler will be able to seek out legal parking.

The better shorebound spots include Garvies Point, Tappen Beach and Pier, Crescent Beach, and most of all Dosoris Creek. Dosoris Creek, from which brackish water flows into the harbor, also washes in various kinds of small baitfish as well. These baitfish become prime targets of blues, bass and fluke. In fact, if you get there in the early morning on a dropping tide, it is not uncommon to see blitz-like conditions of predators feasting on the fry.

Moving out along the west side are two prime hot spots, Motts Point and the Elephant Herd. These two areas are positive blackfish spots, with similar, if not more prolific, structure than Execution Light. The same baits—green crabs and sand worms—will work well, especially in October and November.

PROSPECT POINT
Located on the western outside tip of Hempstead Harbor, Prospect offers anglers a sandy bottom, which is great for fluke action. July and August will be your best timeframes, as the ledges will be packed with sand eels and other baitfish that fluke love. Try working these ledges on the dropping tide and you'll be sure to score with keepers for the dinner table.

EXECUTION LIGHT
Some say Execution Light received its name during the Revolutionary War when the British used the Light as an execution spot, shackling prisoners there at low tide and allowing them to drown on the incoming water. In actuality, Execution received its name for the many boats that struck it and sank during dense fog. As for fishing, the area is a prime blackfish haunt in the early spring and fall, as the broken bottom makes for a tog delight. The structure or broken bottom allows an easy hiding place for blackfish, plus offers a steady bait supply. Typically, green crabs will be your best bait, but sand worms will account for action as well.

WESTERN SOUND
The Western Sound is chock full of opportunities for recreational fishermen. Beginning with an early season showing of flounder and fluke, followed closely by blackfish and chopper blues, the Sound is an aquarium of fish.

In speaking with Capt. Rich Tenreiro, owner of R&G Bait and Tackle and co-host of "Northeast Angling," a local television show dedicated to fishing in the Northeast, Rich feels anglers can score with trophy fish throughout the season. In fact, Rich bested a 52-plus pound striper in April of 2004! But stripers aren't all you can catch.

As for access, this area of the Sound is limited for shorebound anglers, but boaters can enjoy a wealth of opportunities. Some of the access points include Bar Beach in the Town of Hempstead, Manorhaven Beach, and ramps on City Island and Glen Cove. From any of these access points, you can explore the entire Western Sound with ease.

Northeast Angling co-host Capt. Andy LoCascio unhooks a Western Sound chopper, just prior to its release.

For beginners, Little Neck Bay is the first spot anglers will see action. This bay, rich with dark mud flats, heats up quickly in the spring, spawning life in the way of small baitfish and the like. Anglers can easily catch flounder here, but the striper fishery is by far the best bet in this area. One of the better spots in Little Neck is Peterson's Cove. Anglers should anchor up as the tide rises in the 5 to 6-foot depths, right at the edge of the flat.

Moving a bit west is the famed Throgs Neck Bridge. Although anglers must beware in this area of frequent tanker and commercial traffic, the action can be quite good at times. As bait filters out from the west, sharp ledges and drop-offs make great ambush points, especially for stripers.

Over at City Island, this area is home to some of the finest bluefish action anglers could want. Tangling with chopper blues in the teen class is quite common. Beginning in late April, early May, massive schools of bunker begin to form in the No Nations and Beldan Point areas. The Beldan Point area is made up of two large reefs, and is a bunker "hang" that brings blues on their tails!

As we move east, the next up on anglers list should be the Manhasset Bay area. This bay, which is again very shallow towards the back, offers a deep hole, tons of bait and ample structure. The back portion of the bay, rich in juvenile baitfish, makes an ideal area for live-lining bunker for stripers. Although some larger fish can be caught on topwater plugs, most of this action will be on school-size bass. On the west side of the bay is Alan King's house, which is directly across from Plum Point. This area is loaded with rocks and ledges, making it an ideal spot for blues and bass. The east side is sandier, but has ample supply of docks, all of which hold stripers as well. If you want bluefish, however, anchor up off Plum Point in the 50-foot hole and throw fresh chunks. Year after year, this hole produces teen size blues. As you leave Manhasset, to the west is Hewlett Point, a great outgoing water fluke spot. To the east is Barkers Point, which offers a reef, and holds both bass and fluke.

Almost directly in front of Manhasset Bay is Hart Island. This island used to be an active prison, but has since succumbed to vacancy for the most part. It does have some history, however, in that it was also the cemetery for prisoners. Today, in fact, the cemetery (Potters Field) is still used for John Doe burials. Back to fishing, the east and west side of Hart offers a swift current and ample structure in the form of rocks that divert current, again making easy ambush points. This is also a good area at low light—dawn or dusk—for throwing topwater plugs.

Next up is Huckleberry, located northeast of Hart Island, about two miles away. Huckleberry is known as a blackfish haven, with peaks and valleys from 10 to 80-feet deep. Anglers dunking green crabs have scored here with tog to 10-plus pounds year after year. In fact, from Huckleberry to points east on the Connecticut side of the Sound, there are tons of blackfish hangs.

3

MONTAUK—A SURFCASTER'S PARADISE

Although Long Island is home to many surfcasting opportunities, Montauk—"Mecca" to dedicated surfcasters—is the most sought-out area on the island. Montauk offers a wide array of opportunities for casters, all within easy walking distance of most parking. And, if you purchase one of the three permits—East Hampton, NY State or Suffolk County—that allow beach vehicle access, your casting can be done within reach of your buggy.

The action in Montauk begins in early May, and will last through Thanksgiving, sometimes even later. However, if you were going to target Montauk from the surf line, your best timeframe would be the fall—September through November.

Mark Malenovsky caught this 64-pounder, one of the largest stripers taken in recent years, under the famed Lighthouse on a yellow Gibbs bottle plug.

In the fall, as bait begins to migrate south and east from New England and out of the Long Island Sound, stripers and large blues will be your main quarry. These opportunistic feeders will thrill anglers of all ages with aerial displays, and all-out blitzes that can last for hours! Let's take a walk around Montauk and see what we can find in the way of fishing opportunities for the shorebound angler.

UP FRONT

When you hear anglers talking about "Up Front" they are referring to the area directly under the famed Montauk Lighthouse, and the areas just northwest—Scott's and the Bluffs, and the area southwest—Turtle Cove and Browns.

These areas are easily accessed and hold a ton of fish on either the outgoing or incoming tide. For beginners, the Lighthouse proper area is not the place to fish. The rocks under the Light can be treacherous, and landing a fish there can be quite challenging. However, the area just west on both the north and south side offer relatively easy access. For complete novice anglers, you are better off staying in the Turtle Cove area. This area has deeper water, but a sandy beach for firm footing. If you have surf fished and are fairly comfortable on a rock or rough terrain, then the north side, or farther west on the South Side, will offer rocky perches.

NORTH SIDE

Beginning just west of Scotts (right next to the Light) are the bluffs, followed by a cove that plays host to famed Weakfish Rock. Continuing west, there is Jones Reef, False Bar, North Bar, Clarks Cove and then Stepping Stones.

For all of the aforementioned areas, I like to fish the dropping current, where the water movement has your lure moving to your right. The main staple in the lure department is Gibbs Pencil Poppers and Andrus Bucktails by day, with Super Strike Darters, Needlefish and bucktails after dark. If blues are around, tins will come into play as well. And, if you really want to target a cow bass—35 pounds or larger—nothing beats a live squirmy eel! Fished like a lure—cast and retrieved slowly—a live eel will account for banner catches, especially in the fall. Back to artificial lures, there have been times, year after year, where anglers are overwhelmed by action casting hunks of plastic. This is especially true when large baits like baby weakfish, bunker or any of the herring family arrive.

SHAGWONG POINT

Staying on the north side of the Light, approximately three miles west is Shagwong Point. Shagwong can be accessed via foot, but is better run in a buggy. The access point is the Suffolk County Park on East Lake Drive. After hitting the beach, the point is about two miles. You can walk from the parking lot, but soft sand makes for a real hike.

Nicknamed "Shag," this area also produces well throughout the fall, with daily raids of blues a common sight both days and evenings. As the fall progresses, stripers will make up the bulk of these raids, with some larger fish in the mix as well. Currents at the tip of Shag are quite strong, and force bait to be tossed and tumbled, making for an easy dinner.

The best fishing opportunities here are after dark or at first light. In either case, the outgoing tide seems to produce better than the incoming. If you can combine the outgoing with a hard northwest wind, you could be in for the time of your life. Several years ago, we had non-stop action here for hours with bass over 25 pounds! The fish were on herring, which had come very close to the beach. Although none of us could cast very far because of the wind, virtually every caster on the beach walked away with a happy smile after beaching a fish!

SOUTH SIDE—EAST

Moving back to the South Side, the Camp Hero State Park area is open to all by day for small fee attached and there is parking for about 50 to 75 vehicles comfortably. If you opt to purchase a New York State Camp Hero Permit, then you will also have nighttime access to the area.

From Camp Hero, you can make the rather steep walk down the bluffs to several areas. The area directly below the parking area is called the Browns. Moving west, you come to the Sewer Pipe area, then Kings Point, and then Caswells is the following point. Caswells is at least a one-mile hike, but will give you solitude if that is what you want. All of these areas will produce on the incoming or outgoing tide, but I prefer the incoming.

SOUTH SIDE—WEST

Continuing west, there are several open sand beaches, beginning with the ones right behind the town of Montauk. Farther west you have the town beaches of East Hampton, followed by Hither Hills

State Park and Napeague State Park. All of these beaches are drivable with the right permit—NY State or East Hampton—depending on the beach.

These beaches offer anglers a chance at solid action both day and night, with daily raids in the fall fairly common. The key to these beaches is the dropping tide and light southerly winds or north winds. A northeast wind is probably best for quality and quantity when the fall arrives. This push of cool water and air gets baitfish moving along the open beach, with bass and blues hot on their tails.

LOCAL LONG ISLAND WRECKS

Most anglers relate to wrecks as far away places only large boats can fish. Off Long Island, there are a ton of pieces, all within range of the smaller charter or private boat. These pieces hold dolphin, bass, sharks, blackfish, and a plethora of others. In this section, lets explore some of the more famous Atlantic wrecks, and look at a handful of Long Island Sound pieces.

For info on these wrecks, I picked the brain of well-known offshore angler, Captain John Raguso. Capt. John runs the *MarCeeJay* out of Bay Shore, and is also a premier writer for *The Fisherman* Magazine. Capt. John's knowledge of these wrecks will enlighten even the most savvy angler.

THE SOUTH WRECK

The South Wreck is a relatively unknown little hideaway that's only a short four nautical-mile hop south of Moriches Inlet, which is where it gets its name. This semi-secret wooden wreck, known to locals simply as the South Wreck, does not appear in any of the commercial wreck charts or shipwreck books, so you can bet that only a few of the regulars out of Moriches ever fish it. As a result, this structure usually has some form of sea life on it the majority of the time.

According to Capt. John Raguso, "The South Wreck will certainly tax your skills as a wreck angler and attempting to anchor over its low-lying structure is probably best left to the intermediate-to-expert sinker bouncers. Whenever it's late in the day (5 to 6 P.M.) and I'm bringing my *MarCeeJay* back in through Moriches inlet from a fishing excursion somewhere out east, I'll normally reserve at least 15 minutes or so to drop a few clam or squid baits over the structure and see what's happening. Since the wreck only rises up roughly three or four feet from the seabed in its highest spots, you've really got to watch your electronics."

There are two distinct high spots on this piece, with the remainder a scattered rubble field, about half the size of a football field. Other species encountered on the wreck will include football tuna, as well as hordes of ravenous bluefish, so just about anything's possible, including occasional contact with makos and white marlin in season.

As for activity, anglers can expect to find a good population of ling, sea bass, and fluke, all of which will make a great dinner. Drift the edges of the wreck with bucktails tipped with squid or large oily fillets from blues or bunker for fluke. For the typical bottom dwellers, use clam or crab baits on a hi/lo rig close to the bottom. For this angling, anchor up, but be aware, this wreck is only good for one to two boats. If guys are already on the piece, pass it and hit it another day.

SS *CONTINENT*

On Saturday night, January 10th, 1942, the SS *Continent* and its cargo of vegetables, produce and assorted meats went to the bottom of the Atlantic. About four miles south of Scotland Lightship, tragedy struck as the ship collided with the 8,000-ton Tidewater Oil tanker *Byron D. Benson*. The 465-foot long Tidewater tanker delivered a crushing blow to the diminutive freighter, and the *Continent* went down on the spot in a manner of minutes. Fortunately, only one of the *Continent*'s engineers lost his life in the accident, and none of the crew on the *Benson* were injured in the collision.

Anglers can expect to find an abundance of sea bass, blackfish, ling and the occasional summer flounder at the *Continent*'s address. Standing over 20-feet above the bottom, the structure is perfect for holding forage and predators alike. In the fall, football tuna are an added bonus, as bonito, false albacore and school bluefins can be found in the general neighborhood, depending on bait supplies and water temps. Due to the wreck's proximity to deeper water and the Mud Hole, medium and giant bluefin tuna will thrill an angler by spooling his reel!

The *Continent* is easily located (Loran C position- 26884.7/43637.4). As stated earlier, it rises at least 20-feet off the bottom, and is in 130-feet of water. The wreck is located less than one nautical mile northwest of the BA buoy, and slightly to the south of the 17 Fathoms fishing grounds.

The wreck is great for Long Island anglers out of the Rockaways and Jones, but is also favored by the Jersey boys from Sandy Hook, Shark River and Manasquan.

THE 59-POUNDER

The 59-Pounder is located in the general area of the Yankee wreck, situated near the 20-fathom curve, approximately 18-nautical miles south of Fire Island Inlet. According to Capt. John, "I first learned of the 59-Pounder wreck about 20 years ago, while anchored up over the *Yankee*, sharing the wreck with a few other local boats. I spotted a party boat off in the distance, which bore the unmistakable lime-green and white colors of the Freeport-based Capt. Al, hunkered over a spot situated approximately two miles or so to the northwest. I wondered out loud what he was doing there. My closest neighbor, who was roughly 75 feet off of my starboard side, shouted back, 'Old Al must be over the 59-Pounder, catching some sea bass and ling on his afternoon run. He makes the same tour along these wrecks almost every afternoon around this time. He does pretty well, too.'

The wreck rises off the bottom six to seven feet, in 110-feet of water, with the majority of the rubble and debris keeping a low profile. Capt. John also said that the 59 Pounder appears to be a wooden barge or small schooner, based on the strength of its return signal on the echo sounder and its overall shape. Similar in size to the *Continent*, the 59-Pounder is only good for one large party boat, or two smaller vessels.

The 59-Pounder is relatively small, with low lying structure that the average wreck angler might find hard to pinpoint and even harder to anchor over with a wind and sea running. According to reliable rumors the 59-Pounder got its name from an old south-shore skipper who pulled a 59-pound cod off of its structure when it was still a household secret among the sinker-bouncing fraternity.

The wreck plays host to a good supply of cod, ling, tog and sea bass. For real offshore aficionados, anglers have also wrestled with mako shark close to 300 pounds and giant bluefin tuna close to a 1000 pounds! This 20-fathom area, with its wealth of concentrated shipwrecks, makes for extremely fertile fishing grounds for both bottom dwellers and migratory species like sharks and tuna.

YANKEE WRECK

Located 16 nautical miles south of Fire Island Inlet at N40-20.006 W73-16.474, the *Yankee* wreck is directly on the 20 fathom curve, which plays host to a migratory highway for many pelagics during the summer months. According to Capt. John Raguso of the *MarCeeJay*, shark action is consistently good here from June through the end of October, with many 300-pund mako and thresher sharks falling for well-placed chumslicks and mackerel or bluefish baits. For bottomfish anglers, cod, pollock, sea bass, ling, and blackfish will all be found at various times from spring through fall. John also said that, "Depending on the quality of water, warm core eddy spinoffs and forage opportunities, bluefin tuna, their smaller football cousins (skipjack, little tunny and bonito) and the occasional yellowfin can be caught within casting distance of the wreck." Anglers from the western NY Bight sailing from Jones, Debs, and Rockway inlets will also find the *Yankee* wreck a short hop from shore, offering quality fishing less than an hour from home port.

THE DODGER

Located approximately 10 nautical miles south southeast of Fire Island Inlet, the Dodger is in a crowded neighborhood of wrecks including the Reggie, *Hylton Castle* and the *San Diego*. The Dodger, along with these other wrecks, are favorites among the Captree party boat fleet. Spring trips will yield good catches of sea bass, blackfish, ling and others.

The Dodger is situated just a relatively short hop to the south-southeast from Fire Island Inlet, resting in 96-feet of water. According to noted diver and wreck historian Dan Berg of Aqua Explorers, "Rumor has it that the Dodger was given its name by an unknown south-shore party boat captain who first found the wreck on the day that the Brooklyn Dodgers won the pennant."

Capt. John noted that in one instance while talking to Capt. Speedy Hubert of the Captree based "Speedy Fleet," Speed said he has been in the business for over 40 seasons and that the Dodger had always been on his wreck list since day number one, so we know for sure that this wreck dates back to at least 1965. Speed's sources lead him to believe that the two pieces of the wreck might be the remains of a tug that was pulling a wooden barge. Speedy remarked that the wreck changes its profile every few years, the function of shifting sands and rough currents that are driven by hurricanes and northeasters that buffet our coastal area on occasion. As such, different parts of the wreck can suddenly open up one season, creating a flurry of concentrated activity, as foraging groundfish that wander from spot to spot find it to their liking and take up seasonal residence.

One aspect anglers should be aware of on the Dodger is its sensitivity to being fished out. The wreck cannot withstand day-in and day-out pressure. If you have fished on it Tuesday, let it sit and hit it again Friday or Saturday. In today's world, however, with so many boats and state-of-the-art electronics, this may be tough.

THE *DRUMELZIER*

Located outside Fire Island Inlet, the *Drumelzier* is situated about 1,000 yards east of the Democrat Point rock jetty. Locals used to call it the "Quadrant Wreck," because the unfortunate vessel's steering quadrant would stick up out of the sand, making for a conspicuous landmark that didn't require any electronics.

According to the Suffolk Marine Museum in Sayville, there are references that tie in the names of the Quadrant Wreck to that of the *Drumelzier*, a turn-of-the-century British tramp steamship. This unfortunate vessel shipped out of the port of New York on Christmas Day, 1904 with a full load of steel and copper cargo in her belly, bound for Le Havre, France, but ran aground on Fire Island's outer bar in a blinding snowstorm only a few hours after clearing New York harbor.

Although the wreck is still just outside the inlet, numerous northeaster storms over the decades since her grounding has pounded this wreck, radically altering her profile over the 94 years that she has rested in 16-feet of water, just south of Robert Moses State Park. The continually shifting sands of Fire Island Inlet have also covered up much of the steel structure that for many years was high and dry and easy to spot from the beach.

The wreck is a bit difficult to find. However, if you watch your recorder closely, and are in the vicinity of 26674.0 and 43754.0, you'll find small rises off the bottom. In fact, Capt. John has located the boliers at times, which rise at least 6 feet off the floor in only 16 to 18 feet of water. The *Drumelizier* was originally 340-feet long with a 44.5-foot beam, loaded with a full cargo of copper and steel ore, so there's plenty of rubble all around to attract blackfish, sea bass, stripers, bluefish and the occasional fluke. Drifting eels near the remains of the *Drumelzier* in the fall months has taken many a trophy bass, I guarantee you.

THE SHANGRI-LA WRECK

Here's a wreck that for years was considered top secret by local anglers. The wreck does not appear on charts, and is situated some six nautical miles north of the Oregon. Despite knowing where it lies, anglers had a real tough time finding it. According to Capt. John, "I stumbled upon the Shangri-La's whereabouts on a shark trip about 15 years back with Babylon Tuna Club angler Pete Nowinski. We had gone out on "one of his last trips" on his 29 Topaz, since he was planning on selling the boat and retiring from fishing. Since he was in a charitable mood, he gave me the numbers to the Shangri-La's final resting spot with no strings attached. What a score!"

Capt. John has fished this wreck a handful of times, but found that the wreck was scattered about a generally low lying rubble

Capt. Joe Magadino and Billy Turnbull both score well with cod while fishing the inshore wrecks and pieces on the South Shore.

field, with just a few high spots rising up anywhere from four to eight feet off the bottom. The wreck is located in roughly 104 feet of water, situated 5.8 nautical miles north of the Oregon wreck and approximately seven miles west of the Walcott wreck. Looking north from the Shangri-La, you can clearly see Fire Island's Great South Beach and Smith Point Park, which are positioned a little over six miles distant. The closest inlet to the wreck is Moriches, which is 8.9 nautical miles to the NNE.

For angler action, cod will be found in the fall and winter months. Lately some sea bass have been found, but they are best sought in early spring or fall. Anglers have also trolled up all three members of the football tuna clan—bonito, false albacore and skipjack—in this general vicinity, as well as the occasional bluefin tuna and dolphin. Makos and blue sharks will also frequent this locale, although they are more likely to travel a bit further to the south, closer to the 20-fathom curve.

THE THREE SISTERS

The Three Sisters almost always plays host to large chopper blues in the 70s. Freeport based party boats would almost always make a stop there, just looking for a pool fish. In fact, the large blues, a staple of a mako's diet, would occasionally be walloped by a mako as well, making for an interesting day.

For anglers based in the western New York Bight, the Three Sisters wreck is located fairly close to home, situated in roughly 80 feet of water approximately 12 miles south of Jones Inlet, in an area that has attracted hundreds of wrecks over the years. The reason for the abundance of submarine structure in this focused area is no doubt due to the frequency of disaster striking unsuspectingly in the heavy traffic of the Nantucket-to-Ambrose shipping lane. Some of these losses were due to acts of war, others to weather, and still more the result of poor seamanship and bad luck. Which one of these caused the demise of the Three Sisters wreck is anyone's guess.

According to noted diver Dan Berg, the prominent part of the wreckage is a large, four-bladed steel propeller and shaft, plus her boiler section, which rises up four to five feet off the bottom. Resident groundfish include cod, sea bass, ling and tautog in season, as well as migrating fluke in the spring and fall months. As fall approaches and the blues return, anglers should not be surprised to find a mako in their midst, creating havoc. The Three Sisters is another of the smaller wrecks, capable of holding one or two boats at most, so if she's on your agenda, get there early, or have an alternate plan.

THE EUREKA (A.K.A. BROADCAST)

Despite being known by various names, the Eureka was discovered in 93-feet of water, probably by some enterprising south shore party boat captain, and somehow picked-up the Eureka monitor, which is one of the names that she goes by on the local Carmark and Capt. Vic's wreck charts. This shipwreck has also picked up a few names over the course of time, among them being the Broadcast and the Broadcoast. Some other wreck books will mark this structure's position as the Broadcast wreck in lieu of the Eureka namesake, so be advised that they are all one and the same.

The wreck is situated 16 nautical miles south of Jones Inlet. According to some of the local divers that frequent this site, the wreckage is probably not a commercial tugboat at all, since there is a complete absence of any towing bits on the structure. In the past, divers have recovered a huge five-foot diameter bronze propeller from the rubble and have also observed the remains of fishing gear in the sandy bottom around the site. Based on this information, it's a good bet that this derelict is really the remnants of some unidentified clam dredge or trawler that disappeared mysteriously 30 or 40 years ago in a sudden storm or other stroke of misfortune.

According to Capt. John Raguso, friend and diver Dan Berg found schools of ling and blackfish hovering over the structure, with most fish going in the 1 to 3-pound range and a few lunker blackfish here and there. Reports of small cod mixed in with the ling, keeping mostly to the bottom structure. These observations, which were made in the early spring, did not uncover any sea bass or fluke, but rest assured, these bottom dwellers will be there as well.

While fishing one of the local South Shore wrecks with Capt. John Raguso, Chris Driwinga boated this 30-pound bluefin.

John also stated that, "Once the marauding pelagics arrive on scene in June, this area eight miles south of the famed Cholera Banks is known to hold a wide assortment of guests, including bluefish, school bluefin tuna, skipjacks, false albacore, bonito, mahi mahi (August and September), small-to-medium makos, blue sharks and an occasional king-sized thresher during the fall months. White marlin have also been known to cruise this area in July and August when water temps and forage opportunities are just right."

THE *HYLTON CASTLE*

The winter of 1886 was frigid. The Great South Bay was so iced-over that deer could walk back and forth across the bay from the mainland. The temperature that January had been hovering in the low-teens for over a week. It was during this cold spell that the British freight steamship *Hylton Castle* began its trek to Rouen, France. The *Hylton Castle* carried a three-masted rigging to supplement her steam powerplant, to aid her in trans-oceanic voyages. Weighing in at roughly 760 net tons, she was also rated to carry an additional 500 tons of cargo, bringing her maximum total gross tonnage up to 1,258 G/T. For some unknown reason, the *Hylton Castle* had crammed a bilge-busting load of 1,400 tons, or 57,880 bushels, of corn down into her holds for the trip across the ocean. A load that would have had a tough time in normal seas was downright silly for rough seas. Around midnight, 80 miles from New York City, she began to lose steerage in the building northeast gale. A steady snow cut visibility down to practically zero, and the *Hylton Castle*'s stern began to get sluggish, as the building seas pummeled the ship and her crew, causing the cargo to shift uncontrollably down below. After two days of pounding the captain decided to head back to New York, but soon the vessel's rudder gave out and the ship became unmanageable in the wild seas. After a treacherous night, with the bilge pumps going full blast all night and jamming with the constantly shifting corn cargo below, the captain spotted the Fire Island Light on the northwest horizon and gave the orders to the crew to abandon ship. Luckily the crew was able to get off of the doomed steamer before she dipped her bow into the waves, raised her stern high into the air and slipped beneath the sea in a vortex of foam. Remarkably, not one member of the *Hylton Castle*'s crew was lost in the disaster.

Working the rusting hulk of the Hylton Castle can be literally a 12-month-a-year prospect, weather permitting. There is a resident population of small cod and two- to four-pound ling on the structure during all but the warmest months. Blackfish will inhabit the wreckage for most of the year, as will large sea bass from mid-April through November.

The profile of the Hylton Castle is that of a low-lying rubble field that barely gets higher than fivefeet or so off the bottom. There are however, two conspicuous spots over the boilers and over the bow that tower up to 15 feet off the bottom. It is over these two spikes that the largest concentrations of sea bass will be caught, especially in the fall months.

Other wreck fish to be found here include pesky bergalls, eel pouts, small pollock and bluefish, when they have an inkling for consuming slow-moving bottom species.

Capt. John Raguso's log book indicates that the wreckage seems to lie in a line that runs northwest-to-southeast, with the rubble taking up about 300 feet of the bottom. If the *Hylton Castle* is supporting a lot of traffic, the *San Diego* wreck is situated approximately two miles to the northeast, so there's always a backup plan available.

THE *IBERIA*

Located in between Jones and Debs inlets, the *Iberia* lies in 55 feet of water and is easily picked up by a good piece of electronics.

The *Iberia* was a tramp steamship built in Scotland in 1881, owned by French merchants who operated out of Marseilles. Like the *Hylton Castle* wreck, the *Iberia* was powered by a single large steam engine that was fueled by multiple boilers. The *Iberia* also had two masts to hoist a few sails when a favorable wind allowed some extra speed. Somewhere off the south shore of Long Island, just southwest of what was later to become Jones Beach, the *Iberia* experienced engine trouble, where the vessel was forced to lay at anchor for three weeks while she made repairs. After being repaired, the *Iberia* continued, only to run into a dense fog during the morning of November 10th, forcing the vessel to slow her speed. Headed straight for her, and unknown to the crew of either vessel, was the big Cunard liner *Umbria*. After spotting the *Iberia* moving in front of her, the captain of the *Umbria* ordered full-reverse, but to no avail. The liner could not stop her headway and her bow crashed into the portside stern section of the *Iberia*, slicing it off completely. The *Iberia*'s water-tight aft bulkhead prevented her from sinking immediately after the collision, but she found her way to the bottom before help could arrive.

Today abundant schools of cooperative sea bass, tautog and pesky bergalls inhabit the wreckage, seeking protection in her structure and feeding on the abundant shellfish and forage that are found there. Although the sea bass action will last from May through October, the larger fish will most definitely be found in the fall months. Blackfish will also frequent the wreck during this same timeframe, but might be found a little sooner and a little later in the calendar's schedule, depending on water temperatures and the fish's migration patterns. The largest blackfish will usually be found at the extreme ends of the season. Ling will also frequent the *Iberia* wreck, but usually as a by-catch, depending on their migration habits and forage opportunities. Anglers working the edges of the *Iberia* with fluke balls tipped with squid will find fish along the edges.

Pelagics such as bluefish, bonito and false albacore are known to cruise the general vicinity of the *Iberia* in the summer and fall months, in addition to holding schools of Spanish mackerel when the surface water temps rise above 70 degrees. Schools of mahi mahi can be found on the surface during warm winters.

THE *IMMACULATA* WRECK

The *Immaculata* rests 18 miles south of Jones and Debbs inlets, and is easily reached by anglers with seaworthy craft in the 19-feet-plus range. For anglers who fish these fertile waters of Jones and Debbs (East Rockaway), there are dozens of shipwrecks to choose from. The *Immaculata* is another name on the charts, but most likely is lower on most anglers' priority scale when planning a day of sinker bouncing for cod, sea bass, ling and blackfish. Most anglers become creatures of habit over time, and if they find a wreck that produces well, usually will not drift far from it. With superb spots like the Yankee, G&D and other more frequented stopover points, all within a one-hour run from these inlets, what would you target for a day's fishing?

Capt. John Raguso says, "The *Immaculata* is not as popular as these aforementioned high-profile wrecks because it consists of a low-lying rubble field that is more difficult for the novice wreck fisherman to locate and anchor over, which in my book makes this site even more desirable, due to the reduced amount of fishing effort. It definitely takes time for the inshore wrecks to get 'repopulated' with new inhabitants, especially when they are on the short list of all the local party boats hailing out of Freeport, Point Lookout and Captree fishing stations. Add a few hundred dedicated recreational wreck fishing craft to this mix and I'm truly amazed that there are still any bottom fish left on these 'big name' wrecks during the summer and fall months."

For more info on the wreck, we checked with Capt. Dan Berg of Aqua Explorers. Being a high profile diver, Dan has info on most wrecks, available through his books, which all anglers should get a copy of! Dan said "The *Immaculata* lies on a silty bottom, situated in approximately 90 feet of water in the neighborhood of the 15-fathom curve that undulates south of the Long Island shoreline."

The wooden framing and ribs of the old barge is scattered about in a general area, with some points rising up to four feet off the bottom, but with the majority of the rubble keeping a relatively low profile of only two-feet or so off the sea floor.

Capt. John revealed, "Although the *Immaculata* wreck is at least 18-miles from the closest inlet and would seem like it should be resting in at least 20 fathoms of water, the uniform bottom of this location is merely 88-feet deep, cruising in the general direction of the Mud Hole west." During the colder winter months, cod, ling and blackfish are known inhabitants of the structure, also resident during the spring and fall months. During the summer, sea bass can also be found here, in addition to some occasional doormat fluke, with both species present on the wreck during their migration periods inshore and offshore in the spring and fall. Pelagic species like bluefish, bonito, false albacore, skipjack, school bluefin tuna and the occasional dolphin will be caught near the wreck during the spring, summer and fall, driven by the availability of forage and their preferred water-temperature ranges. And you can bet that if these pelagic predators are around, the apex predators can't be far behind, with small-to-medium sized makos, blue sharks, threshers and browns cruising the general area at the same time. Since there is such a dispersed rubble field around the wreck, it makes sense to drift the perimeter a bit before anchoring, to determine where the schools of bottom fish are congregating and localizing these spots with marker floats. Once you have found these congregating points, your anchoring job should be significantly easier as you back down and set up near the markers. Be aware that changes in tide or wind direction will usually cause the bottom dwellers to shift their position on the wreckage, so be prepared to move around a little to keep a steady stream of action.

POLING BROTHERS NUMBER TWO

For our last look at local wrecks, we'll head up the Long Island Sound, and check out a barge known to be a haven for a variety of gamefish, and less than a half-hour's run from over a dozen bustling fishing ports that dot the North Shore of Long Island and the southeastern sections of Westchester County.

For expertise in the this area, the info came from an interview with one of the most prominent captains on the North Shore—Capt. John Lowe of the *Dancing Bear*. Although John no longer sails these waters, his years of fishing experience were a tremendous resource, which I will pass on to anglers here!

Research indicated that the Poling Brothers Number Two was sunk in the winter of 1940. The sketchy information that was available indicated that the barge measured roughly 115 feet in length, with an 18-foot beam. According to Capt. John, the Poling Brothers

Number Two barge is now characterized by a tight, low-lying rubble field that stretches roughly 75 feet long by 20 feet wide. Most of this debris is fairly tight to the seabed, rising only two to three feet off the mixed sand and mud bottom. Capt. John mentioned that there is a significant high spot that comes up off the bottom about eight to 10 feet, near one end of the wreckage. This is probably the remains of the barge's pilot house, which was situated on the aft end of the vessel. Although this high-rise section should probably be the focus of your anchoring or drifting efforts once on-site, he did suggest that the low-lying structure often holds the largest fish. It's probably best to give the complete area a closer look with your color fishfinder before committing to one spot or another. Since the Poling Brothers Number Two has broken down over time to a relatively compact profile, this structure can probably hold three or four boats at the most, depending on which way the wind and the tide are moving, so be sure to get there early if it's on your fishing agenda.

From a fishing standpoint, the 52-foot waters of Poling Brothers Number Two resting spot hold a variety of gamefish in season. According to Capt. Lowe, "The best springtime action for blackfish seems to start when the dogwoods bloom, which are coincidental with roughly 52-degree surface water temps, and when the spring forsythias flower, it's time to gear up for flounder fishing." Resident species on this sunken barge include tautog, striped bass, sea bass, porgies, fluke, flounder and bergalls, as well as the occasional school of chopper bluefish. April-through-June are best at this site for blackfish, with the action picking up once again in the fall from early October through Thanksgiving weekend, when the tog usually queue up for deeper and colder waters. Doormat fluke are also a distinct possibility, especially from May through August, when they are most likely to roam the ends of mid-water structure looking for an easy meal.

FRESHWATER HOT SPOTS

Although this book is geared to the saltwater angler, I've fished Long Island's fresh waters happily all my life and can't let this opportunity pass without discussing some of my favorites. So when the urge for trout, walleye, bass or other freshwater species beckons to you, here are some outstanding Long Island locations to try.

Although there are many more freshwater lakes in Nassau and the City limits, these four in Suffolk County are fished more than most, and will provide ample action for both young and older anglers alike. For info on other lakes on Long Island, go to *http://www.dec.state.ny.us/website/reg1/reg1bof.html*.

LAKE RONKONKOMA
Ancient glaciers formed Lake Ronkonkoma. The lake is Long Island's largest, and probably deepest, with some portions over 60

feet deep. Anglers should try to fish the areas less than 15 feet deep, as lower oxygen levels in the deeper portions make habitat slim.

Lake Ronkonkoma is best known for bass, both largemouth and smallmouth, but in recent years the walleye population has become a very active fishery. Walleye stocking began in 1994, to help control the white and yellow perch population. In 2004, anglers caught and released fish to six-plus pounds—quite an impressive walleye for our waters. Ronkonkoma also contains sunfish and crappie, though large specimens are not common.

In 2002 the DEC, in cooperation with the Army National Guard and local bass clubs, partook in the "Lake Ronkonkoma Bass Habitat Enhancement Project." This project involved dropping over 150 hardwood tree stumps from an Army National Guard UH-60 Blackhawk helicopter to eight reef sites on the bottom of the lake. These sites are clearly marked on the DEC lake map.

Overall the lake measures in at 243 acres, with a maximum depth of 65 feet. Present species in the lake include large and smallmouth bass, chain pickerel, bluegill, pumpkinseed, black crappie, yellow and white perch, carp, brown bullhead and walleye. Tiger muskies were stocked many years ago, and most believe they are all but gone. However, in 2004, a 15-pounder was caught on a topwater plug in June, so who knows, there could be a few left.

There are several points of access to Lake Ronkonkoma. Off of Victory Drive there is a DEC parking lot and a concrete boat ramp. There is also a 100-foot handicapped accessible fishing pier located in the Suffolk County Park off of Park Circle Lane on the north end of the lake. Due to its proximity to some of the best habitat in the lake, the fishing pier is highly recommended as a shore fishing spot.

A Suffolk County Green Key is required and seasonal park fees may apply. For more information call the Lake Ronkonkoma County Park at (631) 854-9699 or see Suffolk County Parks.

Directions: Lake Ronkonkoma lies just north of the Long Island Expressway and east of Ocean Avenue in Ronkonkoma. To reach the

DEC boat launch, take Ocean Avenue north to Rosevale Avenue. Make a right onto Victory Drive. The boat launch entrance, marked with a wooden DEC sign, will appear on your left.

Restrictions: Boats are permitted but may only be launched from the DEC boat launch. Electric trolling motors are allowed; gas motors are prohibited. Shoreline access is available as well.

After arriving at the lake, you can easily find the access points. Additional information on the lake can be obtained from Frank or Tony at Ronkonkoma Outfitters, located at 335 Smithtown Blvd. (across from the Suffolk County Park entrance). You can also call ahead for up-to-date info at 866-3-TACKLE.

FORGE POND—RIVERHEAD

Forge Pond is part of the Peconic River system. Forge Pond is one of Long Island's premier fishing spots for largemouth bass. For the last decade, the average catch rate for Angler Diary Cooperators has been about one bass for every two hours of fishing effort.

From the access site anglers can either steer downstream to fish the main pond or upstream to fish the river. The numerous small coves, overhanging trees, and lily pad beds are prime cover for big bass and chain pickerel. A small boat is extremely helpful in reaching these features. Forge Pond also offers excellent springtime fishing for sunfish.

The pond comes in at 120 acres, with a maximum depth of about six feet. Anglers can expect to find a solid largemouth population, with fish easily exceeding the five-pound class. Other species in the lake include: chain pickerel, bluegill, pumpkinseed, black crappie, yellow and white perch, brown bullhead and carp.

To get to the pond, take the Long Island Expressway to exit 71 (Edwards Avenue). Go south and take your first left onto South River Road. The DEC access site is on your left.

Boats are allowed, but the access site will only accommodate a hand-carry boat or canoe; shoreline access is limited.

FORT POND—MONTAUK

One of my favorite fishing holes, Fort Pond offers shorebound access, but is better fished via a small tin boat or canoe. The lake comes in at 192 acres, with a depth reaching 25 feet. I have found the best action to be at the north end of the lake, along the railroad, and among the weed lines about 20 feet off the shore. Crankbaits in the early season have accounted for bass to five pounds, while spinnerbaits during the summer months have worked well on bass in the two to three-pound class. Typical of most Long Island lakes, anglers can expect to find a good population of bluegill, pumpkinseed, yellow and white perch, carp, brown bullhead and walleye, which are currently a stocked fish. The pond is located within clear sight on the north (left) side, just as you enter the town of Montauk. Virtually every road ending will offer some form of access for shorebound fishing. For boat access, make a left on Embassy and then a right onto Erie. Once on Erie, there is a NY State access site on your left.

BLYDENBURG LAKE—HAUPPAUGE

On the page, Blydenburgh Lake, also known as Stump, New Mill or Weld's Pond, is described as one of the most picturesque ponds on Long Island and the least developed. The lake is fed by the headwaters of the Nissequogue River, and contains a variety of fish, but best known for its largemouth bass population. I can remember fishing Blydenburgh back in the late 70s, using artificial worms and bagging fish over five pounds. I fished with a buddy, John Spampanato, who lived close to the lake and knew the hot spots. We found fish where most shorebound anglers would not even think about fishing—and to this day, those spots will remain secret!

According to the voluntary angler diary, cooperators reported catch rates between 0.4 and 1 bass per hour! Fishing for perch and sunfish is also excellent. The shoreline of Blydenburgh Lake is a well-balanced mix of undisturbed fish habitat and access points, all of which offer ambush points for bass.

The lake measures in at 100 acres, with a maximum depth of eight feet. For species, anglers can expect to find largemouth bass, pumpkinseed, brown bullhead and yellow perch. The lake does have varying restrictions throughout the year, and it is best to check with Region 1 DEC for the updated info.

There are two entrances to the park. The main entrance is off of 454 (Veterans Highway) across from the Denison Building in Hauppague and the other is off of New Mill Road just south of Jericho Turnpike (Route 25) in Smithtown.

Although private boats are prohibited, the park does rent rowboats seasonally, usually from Memorial Day through Labor Day, call the park at 631-854-3713 for further details. Additionally shoreline access is available and wading is permitted. The park is closed from dawn to dusk.

6

RAMPS, BEACH ACCESS

LONG ISLAND LAUNCH RAMP LIST
Before heading out to the ramp of your choice, it is still wise to call ahead and make certain there have been no changes.

New York City
Gateway National Recreation Area: Great Kills National Park ramp located off Hyland Blvd. on Staten Island. Open daily April 1 through November 30, there is a $50 annual parking permit fee, ramp use is free. Permits may be obtained at the Ranger station in the park (718) 987-6790. The park has eliminated the special, cartop ramp access.

State Sponsored Ramps: (631) 669-1000 Ext. 286

Freeport: Albany Avenue ramp, located within the Village of Freeport, is owned and operated by the Village but provides free access to all New York State residents. Open daily year round from sunrise to sunset.

Heckscher State Park, East Islip: State owned and operated boat ramp. Located within the State Park at the terminus of Southern State and Heckscher parkways. The ramp is free to all state residents. Park entrance fees are as follows: Beginning 4/6—$6 on weekends only. Beginning 5/25—$6 on weekends and weekdays. Between 6/22 and 9/2—Daily and weekend fee is $8. From 9/3 to 11/24—$6 on weekends only.

Captree State Park, West Islip: State owned boat ramp, located in the Captree boat basin. Deep water, concrete ramp, open year round and is free to all NY residents. Parking fees are as follows: 5/4 through 5/24 $6 on weekends only. 5/25 to 9/2 $6 daily and weekends. From 9/3 to 10/14 $6 fee on weekends only.

Moriches Bay Waterway Access Site, E. Moriches: New addition to the state sponsored ramps that can be accessed via Moriches Island Road to the Coast Guard Station road. Paved ramp for small boats—less than 20'—parking for up to 12 vehicles with trailers. Low tide launch can be difficult, therefore we suggest you plan your launch around mid to high tide periods. Open year round, free to all.

Ponquogue Pier Ramp, Hampton Bays: Located on the southwest side of the old Ponquogue Bridge/Pier facility, this paved ramp will offer access for boats under 20'. The Town of Southampton will oversee ramp use (631) 728-6000. There will be a $25 annual permit required but ramp will be open to everyone year round.

Caution should be exercised when launching boats at or near low tide. The $25 fee can be purchased through parks and recreation for the town. *Use at your own risk.*

Oyster Pond Ramp, operated by the state DEC in East Marion, town of Southold, scheduled to be re-built but free to all at this time. 631-269-4927.

NISSEQUOGUE RIVER STATE PARK

Nassau County

Nassau County owned and operated ramps: (516) 571-7460. The county owns and operates four ramps; all guidelines and fees apply to each.

Bay Park Ramp, E. Rockaway: 1st Ave & Majorie Lane, Bay Park. Nassau County resident ramp permit required, $50 seasonal, $20 daily, non-resident $20 daily. Commercial permit is $400 seasonal and $100 daily. Open year round, ramp closes at dark.

Inwood Park, Inwood: Access via Bayview Ave.

Milburn Creek Ramp, Freeport: Located along Atlantic Ave. in Freeport.

Wantagh County Park, Wantagh: Access via Merrick Road, Wantagh.

Town of Hempstead: (516) 489-5000
Marina West, Point Lookout: Accessed via Lido Blvd. (516) 431-9200. Restricted to boats less than 21', open year round, sunrise to sunset, free to residents and non-residents alike.

Town of North Hempstead: (516) 627-0590
Manorhaven Beach Park: Manorhaven Blvd., Manorhaven (516) 327-3100. $55 annual launch permit required $35 for seniors and

There are many ramps on Long Island, whether you want to fish north, east, south or west!

disabled residents, $8 daily parking fee for vehicle and trailer. Open 24-hours daily Memorial Day through Labor Day. Non-resident fee is $16 daily. You must call security after 11:00 P.M. to launch.

Bar Beach Park, Pt. Washington: West Shore Road, (516) 767-4618. The same guidelines as above except non-residents may use this town facility. The non-resident permit fee is also $16 per day.

Town of Oyster Bay: (516) 797-4114
Roosevelt Memorial Park, Oyster Bay: Larrabee Ave., Village of Oyster Bay. Open 24-hours, year round, Launch fees: $50 resident seasonal, $20 daily. Non-resident—$40 daily. No charge after Labor Day.

Tappan Beach Ramp, Glenwood Landing: Shore Road, Sea Cliff. Same guidelines as above, except the following: open 8:30 A.M. to 4:30 P.M. daily, launching only at high tides due to severe silting problem.

John Burns Park Ramp, Massapequa: Same as above, except non-resident seasonal permits are available for $75, daily—$20. Resident $10 daily. No launching restrictions.

City of Glen Cove: (516) 676-3766
Garvey's Point Ramp, Glen Cove: Garvey's Point Road. Parking for 30 vehicles with trailers. Use of ramp open to non-residents. Permit required. Resident $10 daily, $30 annual. Non-residents $35 daily, $150 annual. Commercial $50 daily, $250 annual.

Suffolk County
Babylon: (631) 957-3000
Tanner Marine Park, Copiague: Kerrigan Road, Copiague. Dept. Parks & Recreation: (631) 893-2100. Open Memorial Day through Labor Day, 8 A.M. to 8 P.M. Resident fee $50 seasonal, $25 seniors. Non-residents $15 daily on weekdays, $25 daily on weekends.

Venetian Shores, Lindenhurst: Located off Grenada Parkway, Lindenhurst. The same regulations and rates as above.

Babylon Village Boat Ramp: Fire Island Ave., Babylon (631) 669-1500. Village residents only, launch permit fee $15 seasonal. Open year round from sunrise to sunset.

Islip: (631) 224-5691
Bay Shore Marina, Bay Shore: Clinton Ave., (631) 224-5648. Resident seasonal permit required: $38. Non-resident daily fee also $38. Ramp open year round from sunrise to sunset.

The following ramps are Residents only:
Maple Street. Dock, Islip: Maple Street (631) 224-5565. Same regs as above except for a 24' boat size limit.

Champlin's Creek Dock, East Islip: Dock Road, E. Islip, same guidelines and fee as Maple Street Dock.

Great River Ramp, Great River: East side of Great River Road. Same as above.

East Islip Marina, E. Islip: Access via Bayview Ave., East Islip. Same as above but no restriction on boat size.

Homan Creek Ramp, Bayport: Paulanna Ave. Bayport. Same as above.

West Islip Marina: Beach Drive, West Islip. Same as above.

Huntington: (631) 351-3014
Ashroken Ramp, Northport: Eaton's Neck Road, (631) 351-3089. Resident's only, $25 annual launch permit fee, $20 beach permit also required. Open Memorial through Labor Day only 8:30 A.M.-8 P.M.

Hobart Beach Ramp, Northport: Eaton's Neck Road, same guidelines and fee as above. Beach permit is required.

Soundview Ramp, Northport: Located along Eaton's Neck Road, Northport. Same rules and fee as above. Open 24-hours per day. Beach permit is required.

Cold Spring Harbor Ramp, CSH: Route 25A, Cold Spring Harbor. Residents only, same rules and fees as above. Beach permit is required.

Mill Dam Ramp, Huntington: East side of Mill Dam Road. Non-resident fee $20. Open year round 6 A.M. to 8 P.M. daily, NO beach permit required. Otherwise same rules and fees as above.

Shirley: (631) 854-4949
Suffolk County Dept. of Parks, Recreation and Conservation: Smith Point North Ramp (Shirley Marina) is open 7 days a week from 6 A.M. to 10 P.M. The annual resident permit is $25. Daily resident use is $5. Seniors/disabled pay an annual $15 fee and $5 daily. Non residents permit is $50 annual and $10 daily and, there is a commercial user fee of $200 annually. Green Key is required. Contact Parks Dept. for information.

Smithtown: (631) 360-7512
Schubert Ramp, Nissequogue: Located at marina on Long Beach Road (631) 360-7643. Open year round to residents only, annual launch permit $30, $7 for cartop boats. Town parking sticker also required and issued free to all residents. Season runs from April 15 through November 15

Kings Park Bluff Ramp, Kings Park: Access via Old Dock Road, Kings Park. Same guidelines as above, except ramp is open ½ hour before sunrise to 1 hour after sunset.

Town of Brookhaven: (631) 451-6100
The town operates seven at the following locations, all require proof of residency and boat registration. The fee for a resident season ramp permit is $60, $35 for seniors or handicapped, $25 daily resident ramp permit. Non-resident ramp use fee: $55 daily.

Corey Ave. Ramp: Corey Ave, Blue Point
Forge River Ramp: Park Road, Mastic
Maple Ave Ramp: Maple Ave., Center Moriches
Pine Neck Ramp: Pine Neck Ave., East Patchogue
Cedar Beach Ramp: Harbor Beach Rd., Mt. Sinai at Cedar Beach
Pt. Jefferson Marina: Main Street, Pt. Jefferson
Stony Brook Ramp: Jane Street, Stony Brook

Village of Bellport: (631) 286-0327
Village Dock Ramp: Bellport Lane, Bellport. Seasonal use. Resident fees: $125 seasonal $25 daily. Non-residents: $200 season $35 daily.

Town of Riverhead: Recreation Dept. (631) 727-5744
Iron Pier Beach Ramp, Jamesport (Sound side). Open 24 hours, year round. Resident use fee $10 annually. Seniors $5. Non-resident use fee: $25 daily, $150 annually. Four-wheel drive recommended.

Town of South Jamesport Boat Ramp, Peconic Bay Blvd., S. Jamesport. Open 24 hours per day, year round. Resident or non-resident must have special $10 annual permit for this ramp only. Seniors $5 annually.

Town of Southold: (631) 765-5182
Norman Klipp Marine Park, Southold: Manhasset Ave., Greenport. Access from 7 A.M.–10 P.M., April–October 31. Resident seasonal launch permit fee: $6. Non-resident $12 daily, $100 seasonal non-resident permit. Guest Lessee $30 per season.

Mattituck Creek Ramp, Mattituck: County Road 48. Same rules and fees as above.

New Suffolk Ramp: 1st Street, New Suffolk. Same as above.

Narrow River Road Ramp, Orient: Narrow River Road. Same as above.

Southold Town Beach Ramp, Southold: County Rd. 48. Same as above but limited to a 20' boat or under, a 4×4 vehicle is required to launch at this ramp.

Goldsmith's Inlet Ramp, Peconic: Mill Road. Same fees and restrictions as Southold Beach ramp.

Village of Sag Harbor: Dock Office: (631) 725-2368
Sag Harbor Ramp: Bay Street, Sag Harbor. Free to all residents, limited parking available. Non-resident daily fee $5. $25 seasonal. Commercial fee $10 daily, $250 seasonal.

Town of Southampton: (631) 287-5717
Bay Ave. Ramp, Eastport: Bay Ave., 24-hour access. Resident annual fee $10, non-resident $150, commercial $300. No daily rates. The following ramps all follow the same rules and rate structures:
Bay Ave. Ramp: Bay Ave., East Quogue
Bay Crest Ave. Ramp: Bay Crest Ave., West Hampton
Birch Creek Ramp: Birch Creek Rd., Flanders
Old Seaplane Base Ramp: Little Neck Rd., Southampton
South Bay Avenue, Eastport
Shinnecock Hills, Inlet Road, west on Cold Spring Pond
West Neck Ramp: West Neck Rd., Southampton
Watermill Ramp: Rose Hill Road, Watermill
Mill Creek Ramp: Pine Neck Ave., Noyac
North Sea Ramp: North Sea Rd., North Sea
East Argonne Ramp: E. Argonne Road, Hampton Bays
Bullhead Bay Dock: West Neck Rd., West Neck
Conscience Point Ramp: Peconic Road, Hampton Bays
Corwin Lane Ramp: Corwin Lane Hampton Bays. Use caution at low tides.
Point Road Ramp: Point Rd., Flanders
Reeves Bay Ramp: Point Rd. off Reeves Bay
Quogue Canal Ramp: Quantuck La., Quogue

Village of Quogue: (631) 653-4498
Quogue Village Boat Ramp: Quogue Neck Lane. Open 24 hours, year round, village residents only, no fees.

Shinnecock Yacht Club, Shinnecock Road on east side.

Village of West Hampton Beach: (631) 288-9496
West Hampton Beach Marina: Library Ave., West Hampton Beach. Free to residents. Non-residents pay $8 daily, $50 seasonal, commercial $50 daily. Open 24 hours, year round.

Town of East Hampton: (631) 324-4143
Residents are free with town sticker, non-residents fee—$50 per season. There isn't any non-resident daily fee.

Alewife Brook Ramp: Cedar Point Park, Alewife Brook Rd., Northwest Harbor
East Hampton Town Bulkhead Ramp: 3-Mile Harbor Rd., East Hampton
Hands Creek Ramp: Hands Creek Rd., E. Hamp
Lazy Point Ramp: off Montauk Hwy., Napeague
Commercial Springs Ramp: Gann Road, Springs
Shipyard Lane Ramp: Springs Fireplace Road, Springs
East Lake Drive Ramp: Montauk Hwy., Montauk
West Lake Drive Ramp: Opposite East Lake ramp

Town of Shelter Island: (631) 749-0291
All ramps are open to residents and non-residents alike, no fees. Open year round, 24 hours. Unless otherwise noted, ramps are located on the road they are named after, most are of concrete construction.

Congdon Road Ramp
Daniel Lord Road Ramp
Simpson Road Ramp

Tarkettle Road Ramp
Thompson Road Ramp
West Neck Road Ramp
Brander Pky. Ramp: Silver Beach Lagoon
North Silver Beach Road Ramp: West Neck Harbor

Private Access Facilities
Old Harbor Marina, Seaford: Adler Rd., (516) 785-0358, open Tuesday through Sunday 6:30 A.M. to 5 P.M. $10 daily, limit 23' boat or under, can't launch at low tide.

Charlie's Marina, Lindenhurst: 910 South Broadway (631) 226-6250. $15 "same day" in and out, $15 one-way.

Mill River Boat Works, Hampton Bays: Foster Ave. (631) 728-6768. Daily fee $20, 26-foot length maximum. New ramp, parking for car and trailer included in fee. Boat storage available as well.

Gone Fishing Marina, Montauk. Located on East Lake Drive, (631) 668-3232. Open for the season from 6 A.M. to 6 P.M. weekdays, 5 A.M. to 7 P.M. weekends. $15 daily use fee.

Silly Lily Fishing Station, 99 Adelaide Avenue, East Moriches.631-878-0247. Open from March 16 to November 15, 6 A.M. until dark. Fees: $20 per day, $200 per season, resident and non-resident.

Beach Vehicle Access
New York State
Four-wheel drive permits are on sale until the close of April and then again after September 15th. The fee allows beach access to Democrat Point, Sore Thumb, Gilgo, Napeague and Montauk (Goff Point included), including Hither Hills. It also allows night fishing access to Sunken Meadow, Robert Moses, Jones Beach and Montauk. Check access points and parking rules on your permit.

The state also offers a "Night Fishing Permit," which allows parking at several state lots. The Night Fishing Permit is $20. For more info, call 631-669-1000 X223.

Suffolk County
The Suffolk County Permit, which allows access to Smith Point State Park, Shinnecock, Cupsogue and Montauk, is available throughout the year for a fee of $75 for residents and $200 for non-residents. The county also offers a night fishing permit, which allows access to Shinnecock Canal and various other lots. For more info, call 631-854-4949.

East Hampton Town
The Town of East Hampton offers a non-resident Four-Wheel Drive Permit for a fee of $200; resident permit is free. This permit gives anglers access throughout the season for virtually all East Hampton beaches. For info, please call 631-324-4143 or stop by the Town Hall on Pantingo Road (Rte 27) in East Hampton.

7

RESOURCES:
PARTY BOATS, CHARTER BOATS, AND TACKLE SHOPS

PARTY/CHARTER BOATS

Below is a list of the major party and charter boats that sail around Long Island. These guys are real pros and put their fares into solid action, trip after trip. The main difference between the two is a party boat is open to all, depending on space, and operates on a first-come first-serve basis. They sometimes sail two and three trips daily. Party boats cater to both young and older anglers alike.

Moving to charter boats, these, although not all, are mostly smaller capacity boats—four to 25 anglers—and are booked by one group or individual set of anglers. No walk on boarding here, you must reserve your boat. There are also larger capacity charter boats that cater to large groups for office, business or group outings where the capacity for 50 or higher is needed.

Party Boats
Montauk
Lazy Bones	631-668-5671
Marlin V	631-668-2818
Marlin VI	631-668-4700
Sea Otter	631-668-2669
Viking	631-668-5700

Shinnecock
Shinnecock Star	631-728-4563

Moriches
Rosie	631-878-3746

Captree
Captain Gillen	631-661-5531
Captain Gregory	631-957-6855
Captain Rod	631-587-7316
Captain Whittaker	631-587-7087
Captree Princess	631-859-8799
Fishfinder	516-287-3704
Island Princess	631-587-6024
Jib Fleet Captree	631-422-3318
Laura Lee Captree	631-661-1867
Speedy Express & Jr. Exp.	631-969-3793
Susan Ann	631-475-3449
Trade Winds	631-419-1212

Freeport
Captain Lou Fleet	516-766-5716
Super Spray II	516-378-4838

Point Lookout
Captain Al	516-623-2248

Lady J V   516-825-5727
Superhawk   516-795-6355

Sheepshead Bay
Big M Express   347-672-8453
Flamingo III   718-763-8745
Mulligan   718-241-7066
Sea Queen   718-332-2423

Howard Beach
Captain Mike   718-738-6148

Staten Island
Atlantis Princess   718-938-3940

City Island
Island Current   917-417-7557

Glen Cove
Sea Otter West   516-676-6361

Huntington
Captain James Joseph   631-424-1253
Noli Eileen   631-544-6414

Port Jefferson
Celtic Quest   631-473-1129
Osprey/Rising Moon Port Jefferson   631-331-4153
Port Jeff Ace/Prowler   631-689-7215

Stony Brook
Lori-C   631-821-1692

Mattituck
Captain Bob   631-298-5522

Greenport
Island Star	631-734-5030
Peconic Star	631-289-6899

Orient Point
Prime Time III	631-323-2618

Charter Boats
Babylon
Lighthouse Fishing Charters	631-834-9520
Ida-Jean II	631-587-1482
South Shore Charters	516-753-1756
Reel Madness Charters	631-661-4520

Bay Shore
MarCeeJay	631-499-0187

Captree
Dixie II	631-859-5195
Fishtale	1-888-347-4825

Center Moriches
Fish On Charters	631-471-4045
Jolly Roger	917-807-2955
No Doubt Fishing Charters	631-581-4043

Cold Spring Harbor
Cold Spring Charters	631-367-4806

Freeport
Sea Rogue Fishing Charters	516-551-2177
Bottom Line	516-488-2288
Codfather	516-868-9073

Gerritsen Beach
Captain Morgan   718-934-3852

Greenport
Capt. Bob IV   631-298-5522

Huntington
Jessica Anne Charters   631-553-2680
Sound Charters   631-242-6780

Mamaroneck
Molly Roze   914-423-6464
Worth the Wake   646-250-4280
The Lady Kim Charters   718-698-6582

Mill Basin
Mixed Bag Charters   718-629-2248

Montauk
Lady J. Charters   631-668-0847
Captain Demaio on the Vivienne   631-324-8820
Daybreaker   631-668-5070
Halfback   631-668-1305
My-Mate   631-329-0973
Sea Wife IV   1-800-308-8969
Miss Mac   516-378-8175
Capt. Mark   631-668-6773
Montauk   631-668-2056
Alyssa Ann   631-668-1051
Capt. Ron   631-668-4630
Nicole Marie   631-831-3217
Elizabeth   631-668-7612
Wee Jack Charters   631-668-1007
King Wayne   631-668-5843

Aisling Charters	917-716-5109
Susie E II	631-523-8862
Debra Ann II Charters	631-324-7883
Adios	631-668-5760
Fisherman II	631-668-2607
Karen Sue	631-668-4011
Rainbow Runner	631-277-4426
Sportfishing Charter Service	800-439-0034
Masterpiece Charters	631-668-3881
Misty	631-859-5043
Sea Turtle	631-725-0565
Misty Dawn II	631-668-4786
Sea Flash	631-673-9510
Jane's Grace IV	914-963-6420
Fishunter	718-740-3781

Orient Point

Rainbow Charters	631-765-4314
Coyote	631-734-6288
Nancy-Ann IV	631-477-2337
Sundowner	631-765-2227
Fishy Business	631-722-9677
Brooklyn Girl	631-395-7055
Grand Slam	631-457-5298
Saxatilis Charters	631-323-1494

Point Lookout

No Time Charters	516-889-1968
Sea Hunt Charters	516-432-8118

Port Washington

LI Fishing Charters	516-978-1634
R & G Fishing Charters	1-888-FISH-HEX

Seaford
Reel Challenge   516-541-2006

Shinnecock
Grey Ghost Charters   516-526-8983
Reel Slacker   631-848-8212
Atlantic Mariner   631-723-1495
Currensea Charters   631-728-3865

Stony Brook
Susan Marie   631-754-3586

TACKLE SHOPS/FISHING STATIONS
Amityville
Comb's Bait and Tackle   631-264-3525

Amity Harbor
Bob's Bait and Tackle   631-842-7573

Aquebogue
Warrens Tackle Center   631-722-4898

Babylon
Augies Bait and Tackle   631-669-9837
Babylon Fishing Station   631-669-4503

Babylon/State Ch.
Frank & Dick's Bait Station   631-587-1442

Bayport
Capt. T's Bait and Tackle   631-472-0302

Bay Shore
Burnetts Marina   631-665-9050

Bay Shore Marina 631-665-1184
Willie K Bait and Tackle 631-665-7414

Broad Channel
Smitty's Fishing Station 718-945-2642 (Rentals Available)

Bronx
Bruckner Pet 718-597-7120

Captree St. Park
Captree Bait & Tackle 631-321-1499

City Island
Jack's Bait and Tackle 718-885-2042

Copiague
Hook Shot Bait and Tackle 631-789-3256

East Moriches
Silly Lily Fishing Station 631-878-0247 (Rentals Available)

Freeport
Donart 516-378-8992
Sea Isle Sports Center 516-868-8855
Woodcleft Fishing Station 516-378-8748
Hudson Point Fishing Station 516-867-9608

Glen Cove
Duffy's Bait and Tackle 516-676-9543
Glen Cove Sports 516-676-7120

Greenport
Greenport Bait & Tackle 631-477-8268
White's Bait & Tackle 631-477-0008

Hampton Bays
Altenkirch Precision Outfitters	631-728-4110
East End Bait and Tackle	631-728-1744
Shinnecock Bay Fishing Station	631-728-6116

Huntington/Huntington Station
Four Winds Bait and Tackle	6310421-1184
Camp-Site Sports	631-271-4969
Dockside Bait & Tackle	631-385-4200
Northport Rod & Reel	631-368-7335

Howard Beach
Crossbay Bait and Tackle	718-835-1018

Jamesport
Jamesport Bait and Tackle	631-298-5450

Kings Park
Terminal Tackle	631-269-6005

Little Neck
East Coast Fishing	718-631-2196

Long Beach
West End Bait & Tackle	516-889-4393

Mastic/Mastic Beach
Mastic Bait and Tackle	631-281-9360
Dick's Bait and Tackle	631-281-9070

Montauk
Johnny's Tackle	631-668-2940
Freddies Bait and Tackle	631-668-5520
Gone Fishing Marina	631-668-3232

Diamond Cove Marina 631-668-6592
Westlake Fishing Lodge 631-668-6252
Uihleins Fishing Station 631-668-3799 (Rentals Available)

New Suffolk
Capt. Marty's Fishing Station 631-734-6852
(Rentals Available)

New York City
Capitol Tackle 212-929-6132

Northport/East Northport
Bowmans Sporting Goods 631-261-6611
Port Deli 631-261-7694
Baitacular 631-261-3474

Oakdale
J&H Sports Outlet 631-244-0600
J&R Sport Center 631-589-9749
Oakdale Bait and Tackle 631-563-5058

Oceanside
Bay Park Fishing Station
516-766-3110

Patchogue
J&J Sports 631-654-2311
Mr B's Bait and Tackle 631-207-2277

Pelham
Al's Tackle Shop 914-738-4589

Port Jefferson
Caraftis Fishing Station 631-473-2288

RESOURCES

Port Washington
R&G Bait and Tackle   516-883-3958

Riverhead
Fisherman's Deli   631-727-4291

Rocky Point
Rocky Point Fishing Stop   631-744-8330

Ronkonkoma
Ronkonkoma Outfitters   631-471-4553

Sag Harbor
Tight Lines Tackle   631-725-0740

Shirley
Smith Point Bait and Tackle   631-281-3766

Sheepshead Bay
Bernie's Bait & Tackle   718-646-7600
Stella Maris   718-646-9754

Southold
Wego Fishing   631-765-5013

Wading River
Wading River Tackle Center   631-929-0364
Xtreme Bait and Tackle   631-929-5077

Wantagh
Causeway Bait and Tackle   516-785-3223

West Babylon
Bergen Point Fishing Station
631-661-5817

Woodside
Peace Token Fishing Tackle
718-565-2376

FISHING REGULATIONS

For up to date fishing regulations, contact the New York Department of Environmental Conservation or one of the local bait and tackle shops for accurate info. Please do this before you fish, rather than after and risk a fine!

RESOURCES

Ken Schultz's Fishing Encyclopedia
McClanes Fishing Encyclopedia
http://www.dec.state.ny.us/
Capt. Segull Nautical Charts
The Fisherman Magazine
Capt. John Raguso's AWS Series

INDEX

59-Pounder, 97

Atlantic cod, 9

Bass, largemouth, 31
   tactics for fishing, 31–32
Bass, smallmouth, 33
Blackfish, 10
   tactics for fishing, 11–12
Black sea bass, 12
Blowfish, 13
Blue sharks, 102, 104, 109
Bluefin tuna, 14
Bluefish, 14
   tactics for fishing, 15–16
Bluegill, 33
Blydenburgh Lake, 114
Bonito, 16
Broadcast, 103
Brookies, 29
Brown bullhead, 30
Brown shark, 109
Brown trout, 29

Cartwright Island, 68
Castle, 61
Catfish (Brown Bullhead), 30
Cerberus Shoal, 67
Cod, tactics for fishing, 10
Conscience Bay, 77
Copiague Hole, 46

Dodger wreck, 99
Dolphin, 102
Dosoris Creek, 84
Drumelzier, 100

Elbow, 64
Eureka wreck, 103
Execution Light, 85

False albacore, 16
Fire Island Inlet, 45
Fire Island Reef, 50
Flounder (Winter), 16
   tactics for fishing, 17
Fluke (Summer Flounder), 18
   tactics for fishing, 18–19
Forge Pond, 113
Fort Pond, 114

Gardiner's Island, 67
Giant bluefin tuna, 97, 98
Great Peconic Bay, 70
Great South Bay, 45
Greenlawns, 72

Hart Island, 88
Hempstead Harbor, 83
Huckleberry, 88
Huntington Bay, 81
Hylton Castle, 105

Iberia, 106
Immaculata, 107

Jamaica Bay, 40
Jones Inlet, 44

Kingfish, 19
   tactics for fishing, 19–20

Lake Ronkonkoma, 11
Layfayette, 55
Lowe, Capt. John, 109

Mahi mahi, 104, 107
Mako shark, 96, 98, 102–104, 109
Manhasset Bay, 87
Matinecock Point, 82
McMurray, John, 41
Mecox Pond, 62
Mikoleski, Capt. Tom, 44
Montauk Point, 64
Montauk, 89–93
Moriches Bay/Inlet, 51
Mt. Sinai Harbor, 74

Narrows, 69
New Mill Pond, 114
Nissequogue River, 78
North Fork, 68
Norton's Point, 37

Panfish, 33
Paradise Point, 72
Poling Brothers Number Two, 109
Pollock, 20
Porgy, 20
    tactics for fishing, 20–21
Porpoise Channel, 77
Port Jefferson Harbor, 76
Prospect Point, 85

Quantuck Canal, 57
Quogue Canal, 57

Raguso, Capt. John, 95
Rainbow trout, 29
Ram's Pasture, 61
Reynolds Channel, 43
Robert Moses Bridge, 47
Rockaway Inlet/Reef, 38
Rose, Bob, 46
Ruins, 68

Sag Harbor Ferry Slip, 72
Sag Pond, 62
Salerno, Tony, 44
Sand shark, 68
Scup, 20
Sea Bass, tactics for fishing, 12
Shangri-La Wreck, 101
Shinnecock Bay/
    Inlet/Canal, 58
Shoerlin, Capt. Judy, 61
Shoreham Pipeline, 73
Smithtown Artificial Reef, 80
Smithtown Bay, 80
Snake Hill, 48
South Wreck, 95
Spanish mackerel, 107
SS *Continent*, 96
Staten Island, 35
Striped Bass, 21
    tactics for fishing, 23–25
Stump Pond, 114

Three Sisters wreck, 102
Thresher shark, 98, 104, 109
Tiana Bay, 60
Tobaccolot Bay, 68
Triggerfish, 25
    tactics for fishing, 26–27
Trout, 28
    tactics for fishing, 27–28

Walleye, 34
Washington Shoal, 67
Weakfish, 27
    tactics for fishing, 27–28
Weld's Pond, 114
Western Sound, 85
White marlin, 96

Yankee wreck, 98
Yellow Perch, 33
Yellowfin tuna, 99

Zachs Bay, 44

Major Fishing Locations on the Long Island Coast
Charts reprinted courtesy of Captain Segull's Nautical Sportfishing Charts.

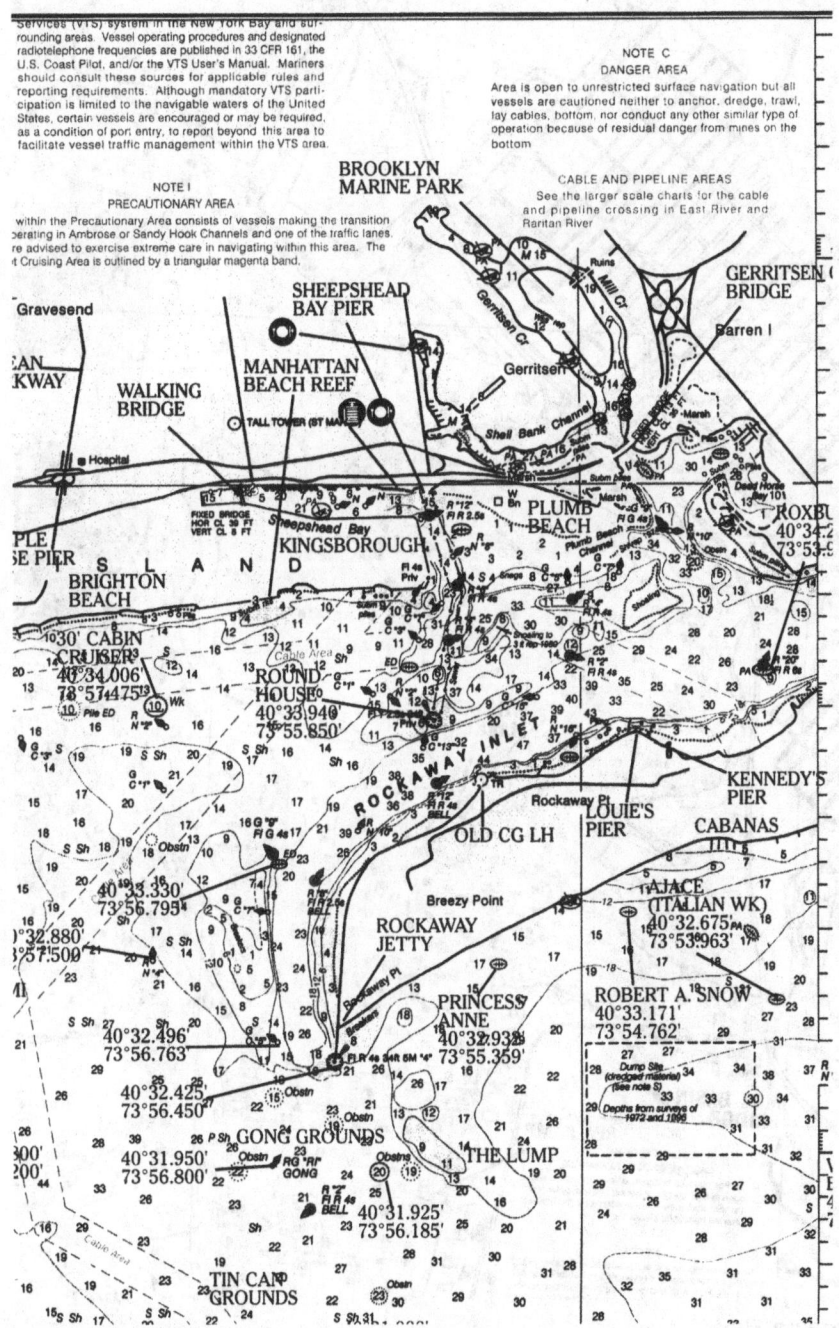

Rockaway Inlet

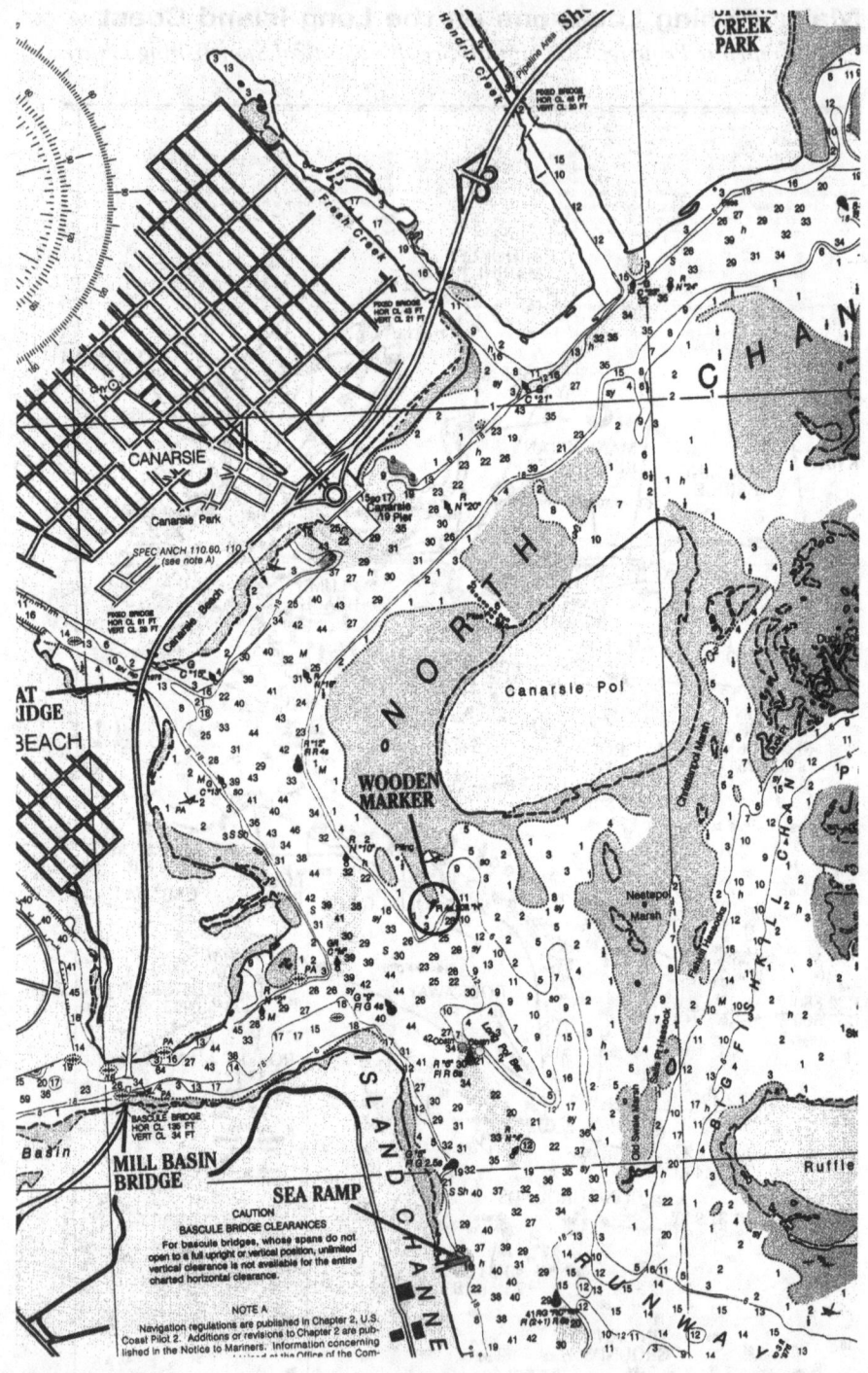

Jamaica Bay

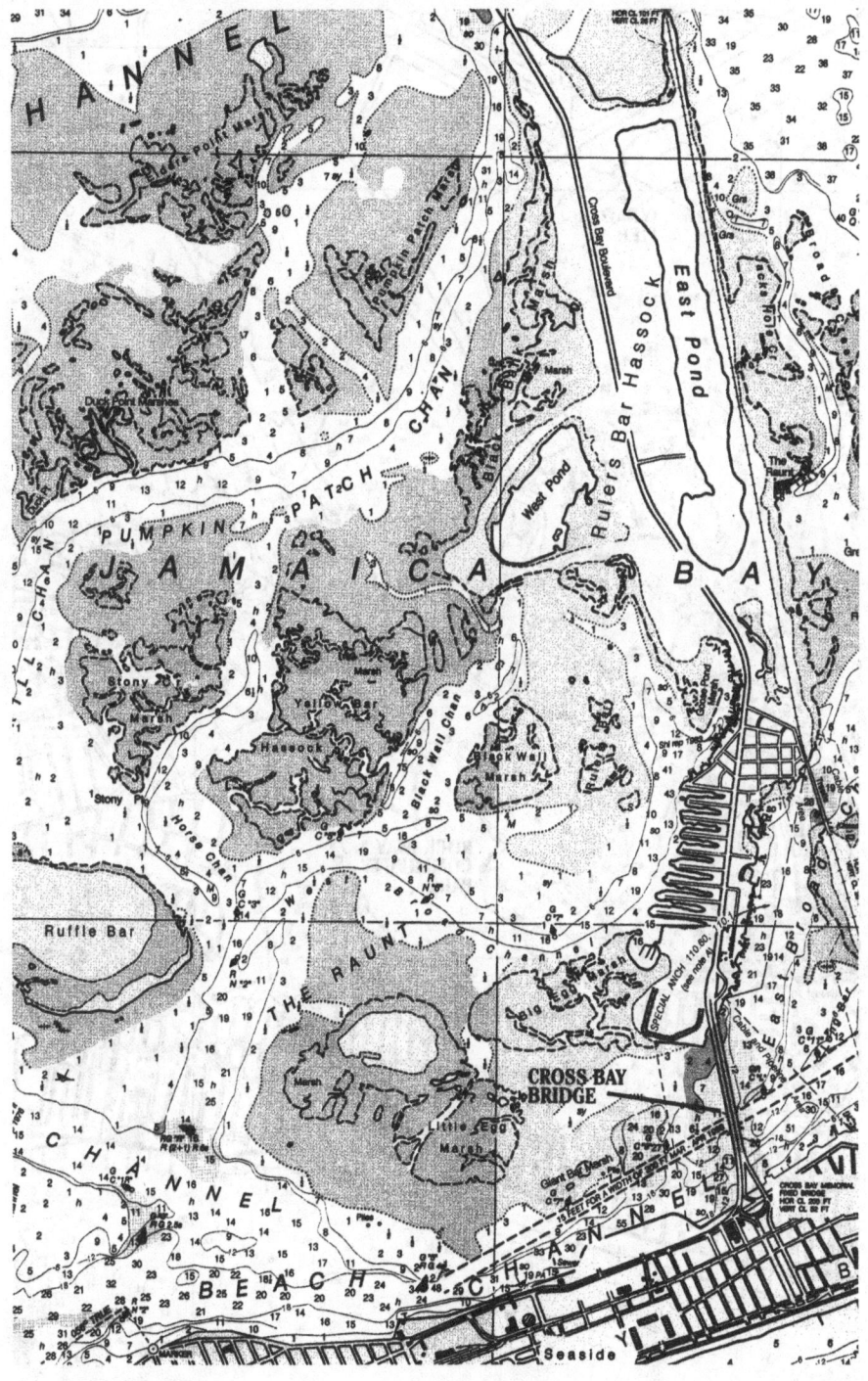

Jamaica Bay 2

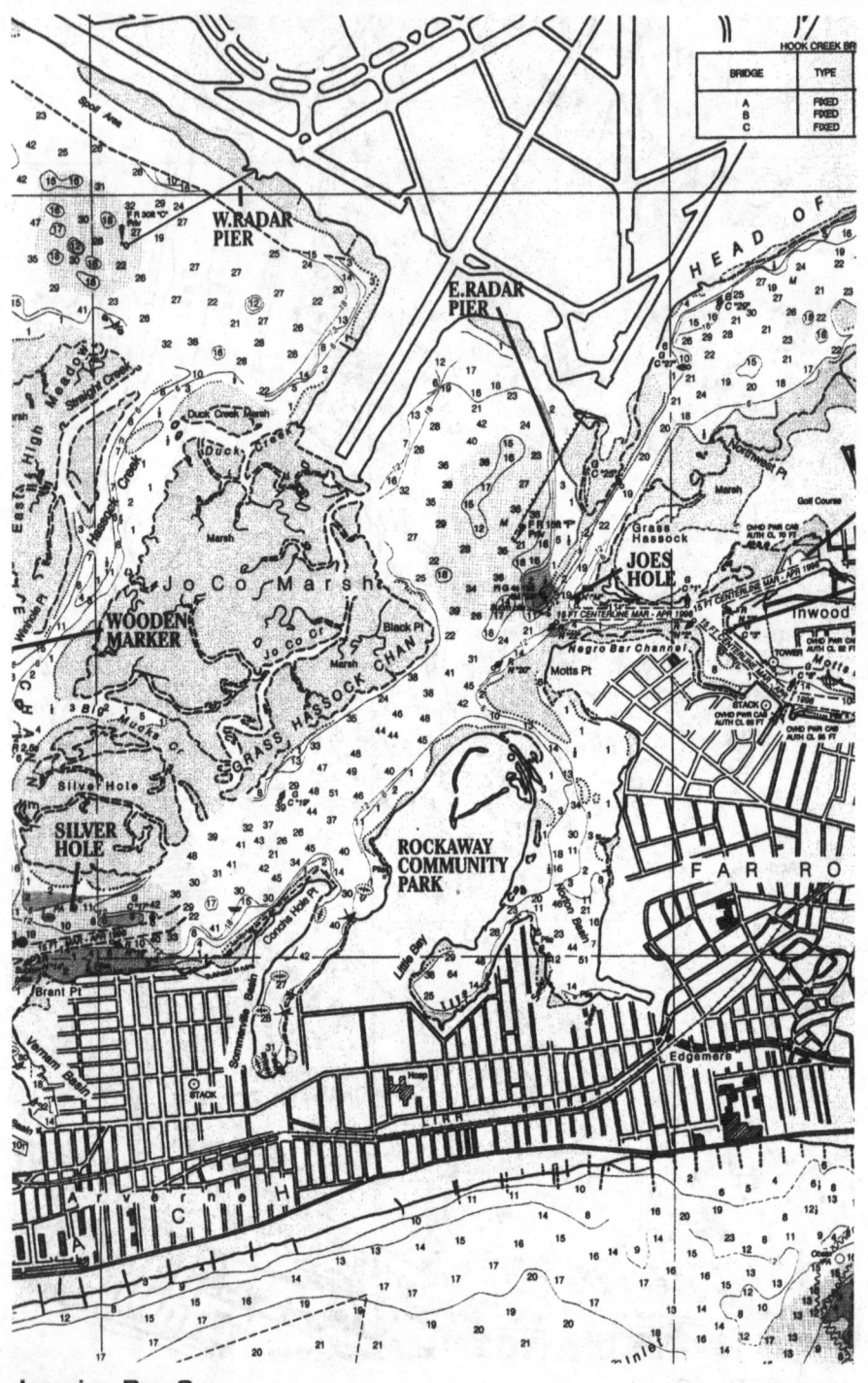

Jamaica Bay 3

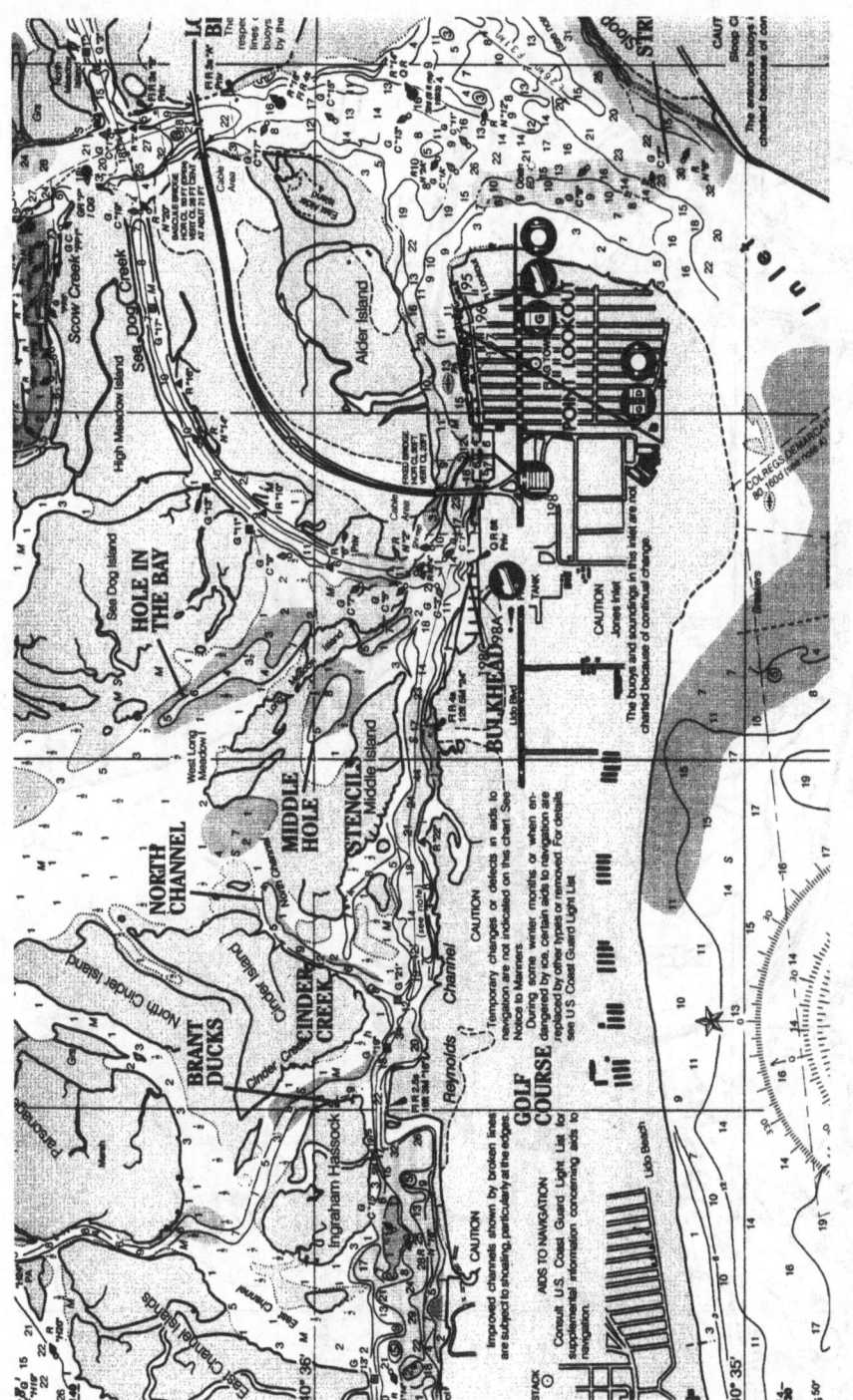

Reynolds Channel

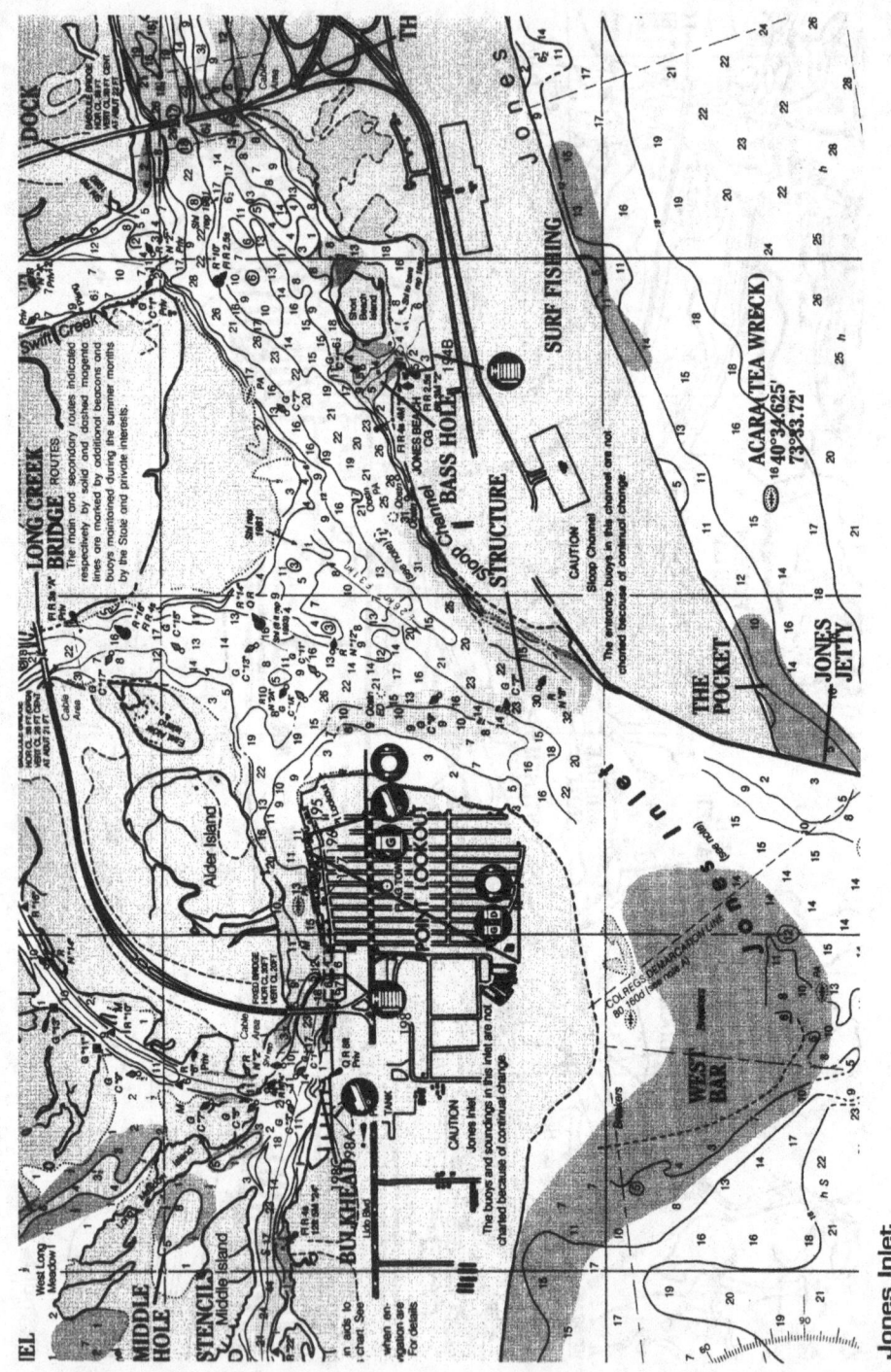

Jones Inlet

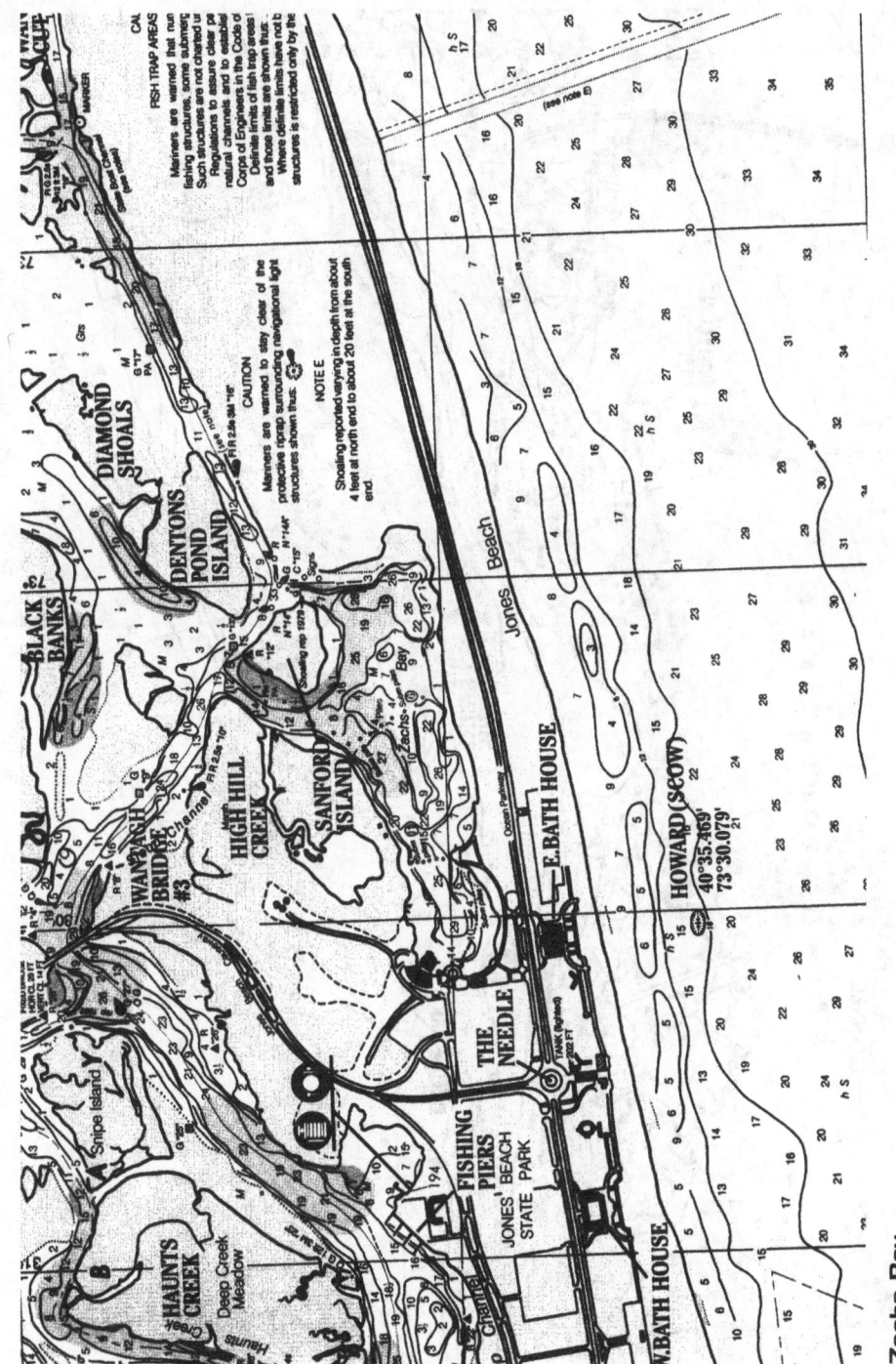

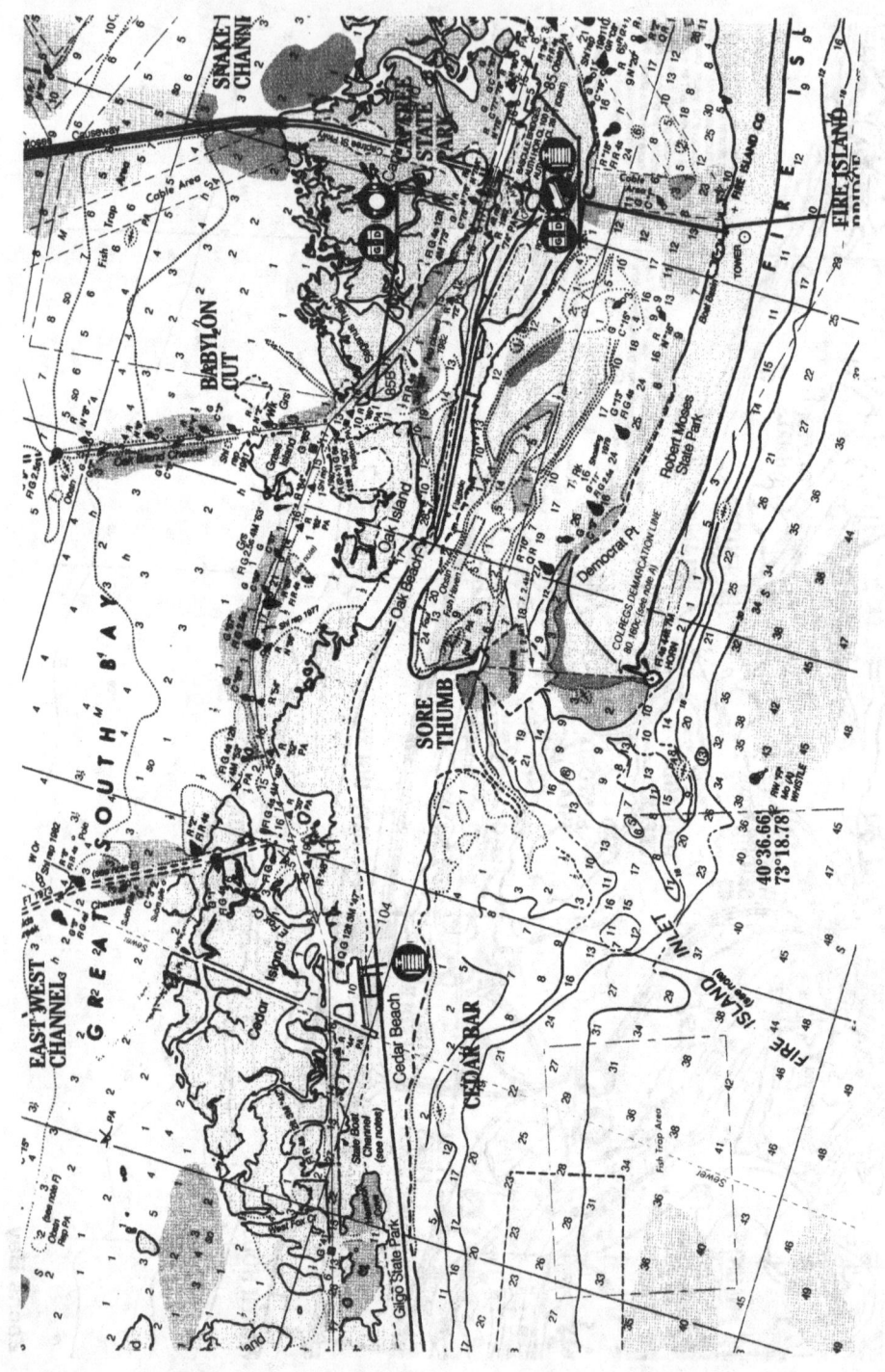

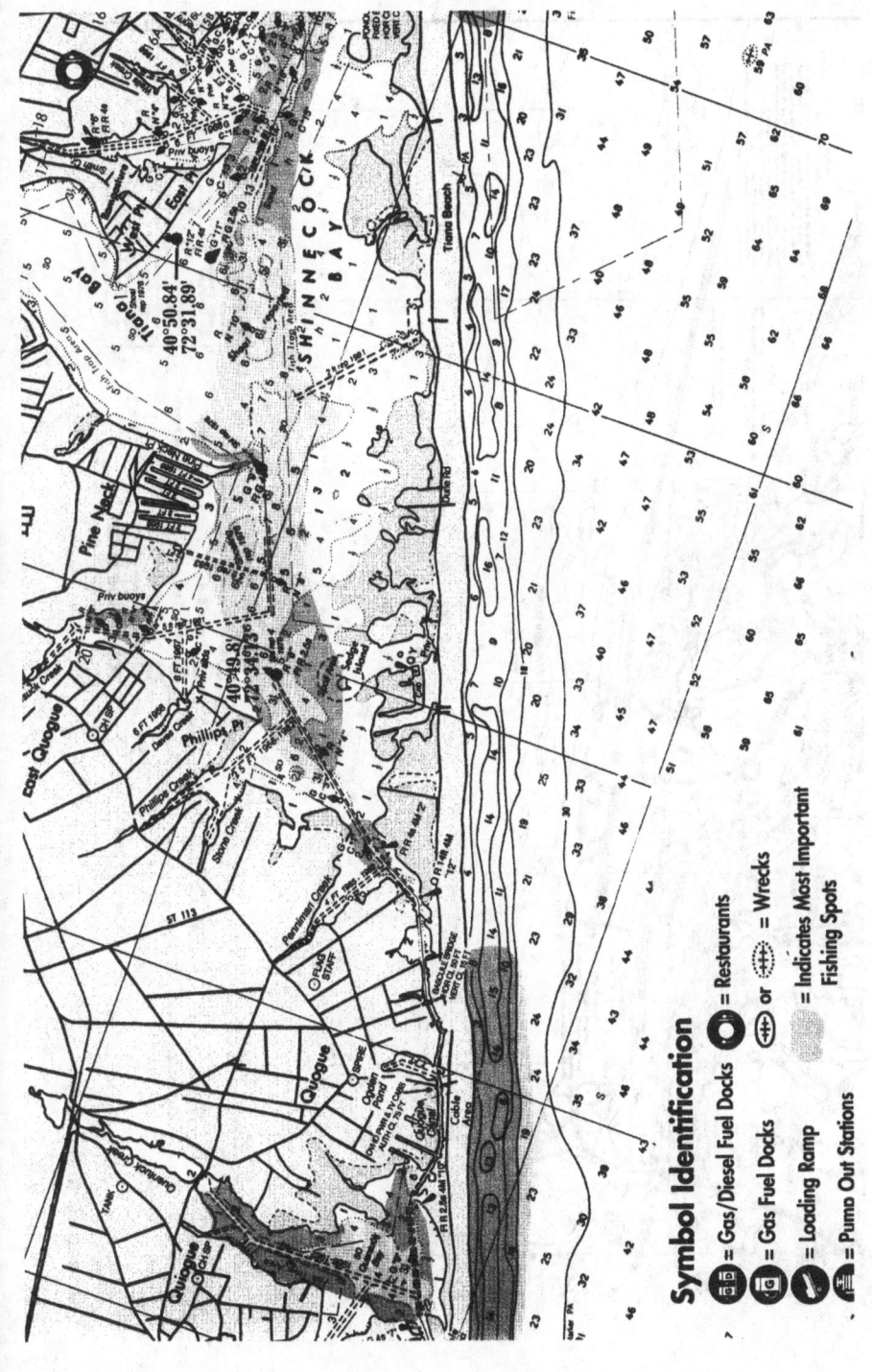

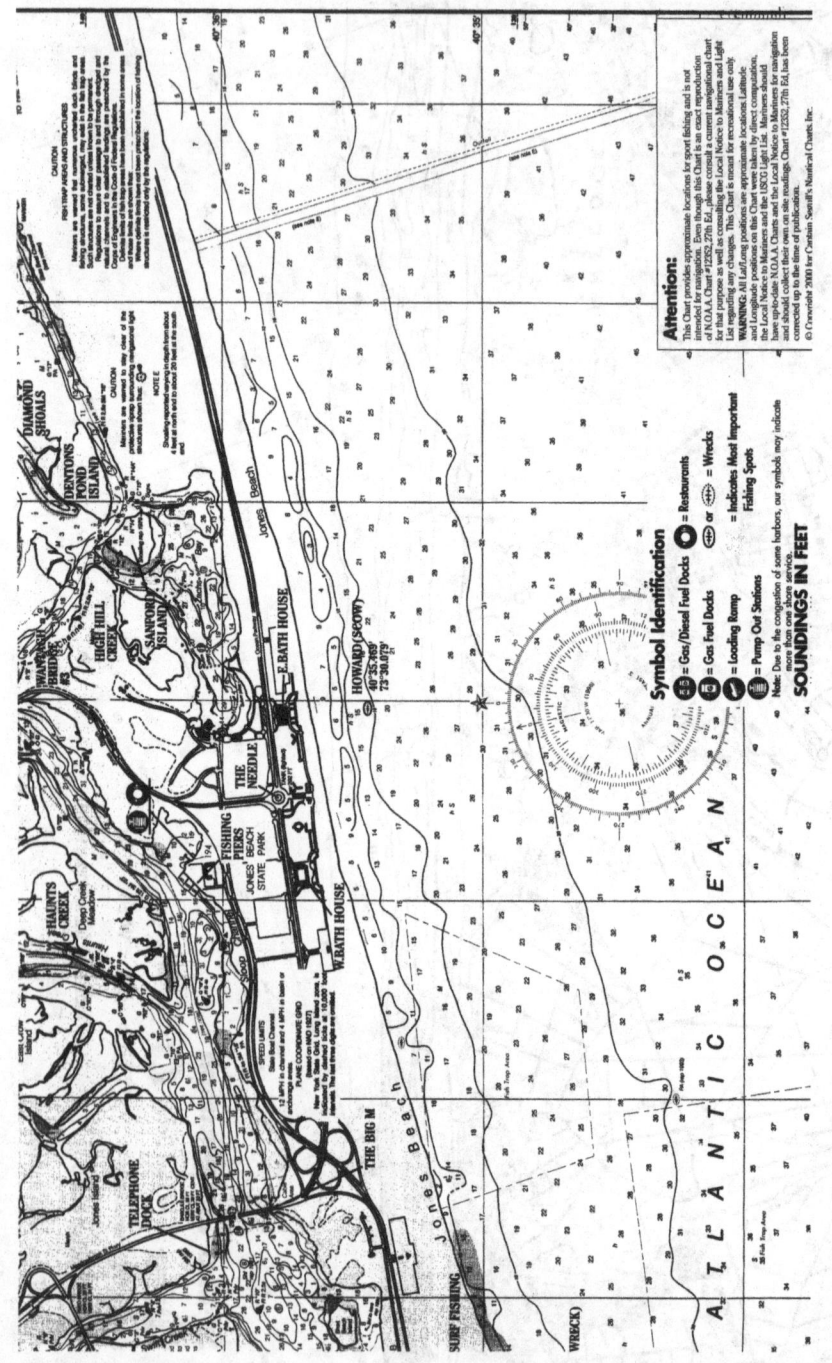

Jones Beach

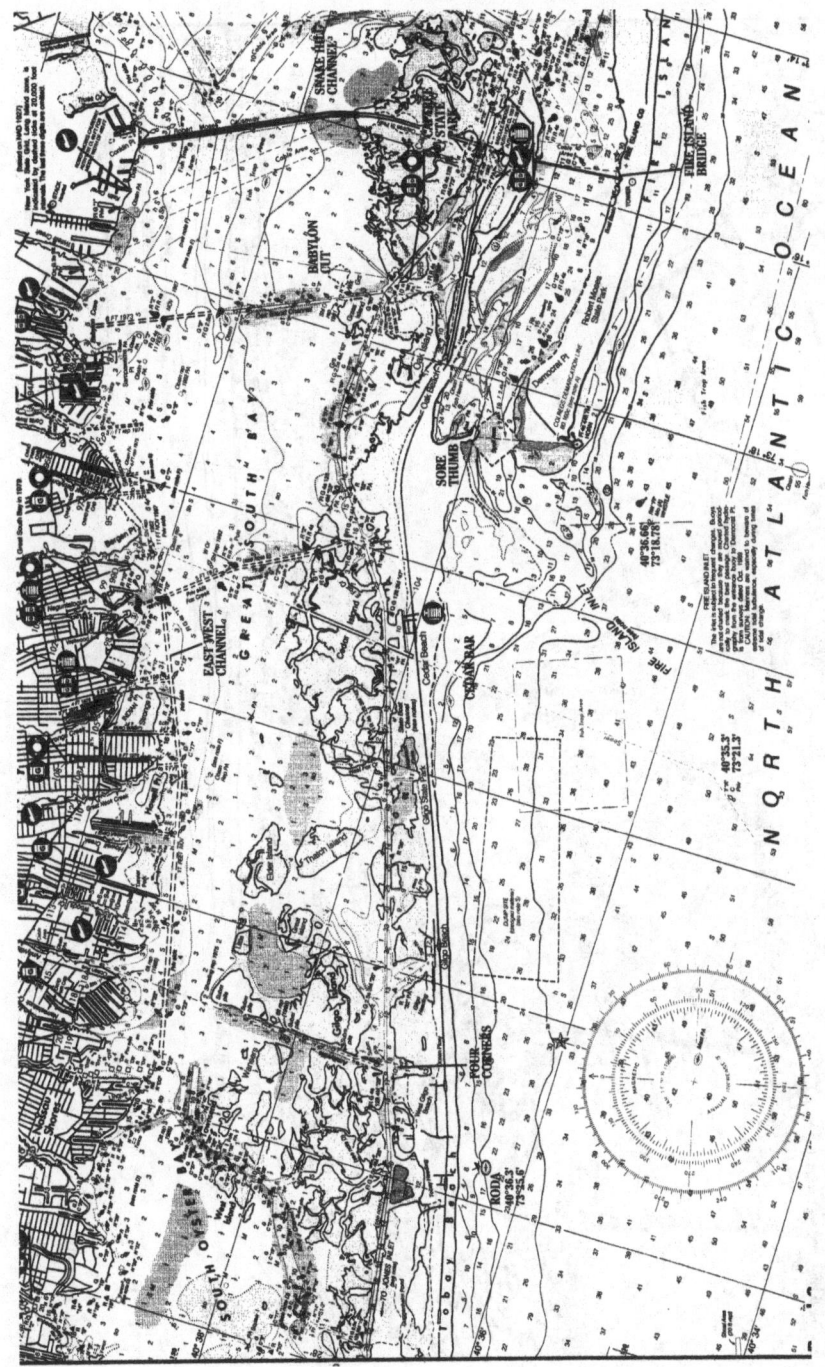

Fire Island

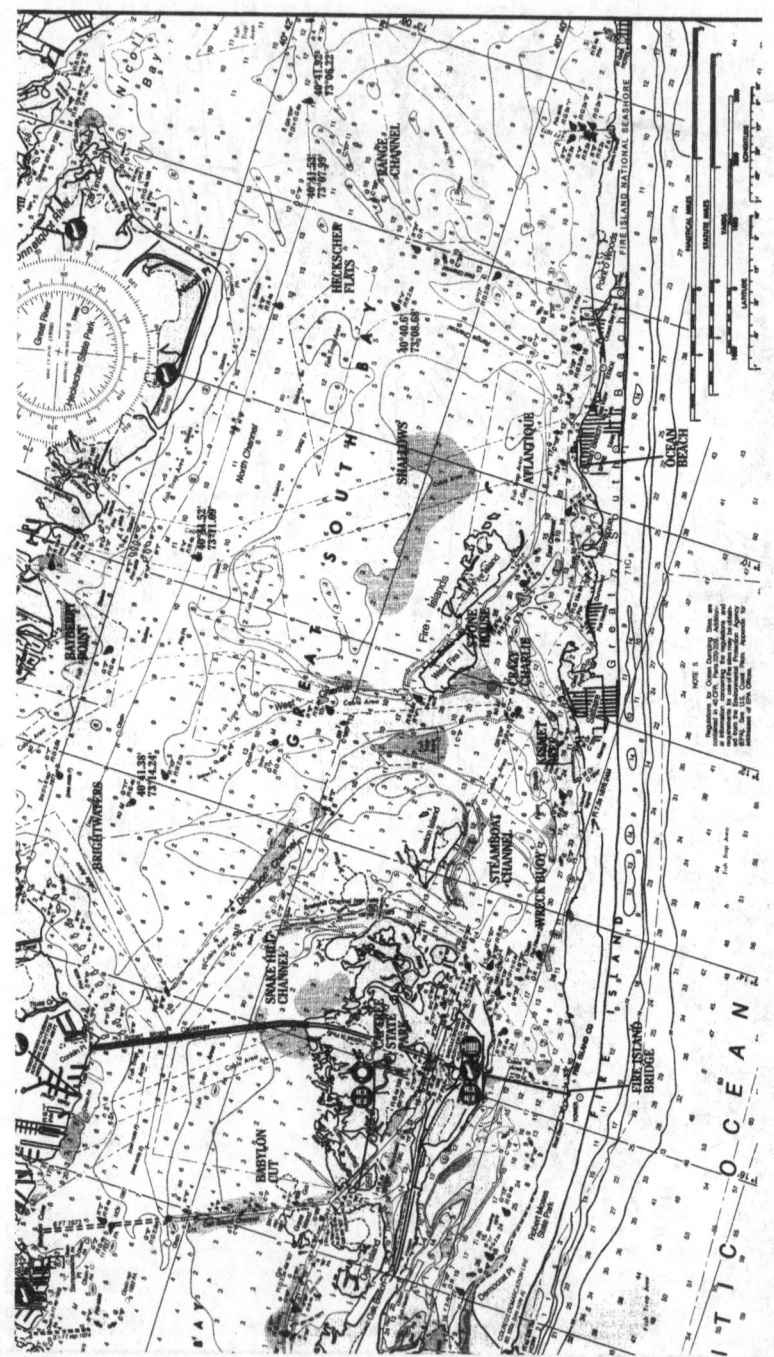

Fire Island 2

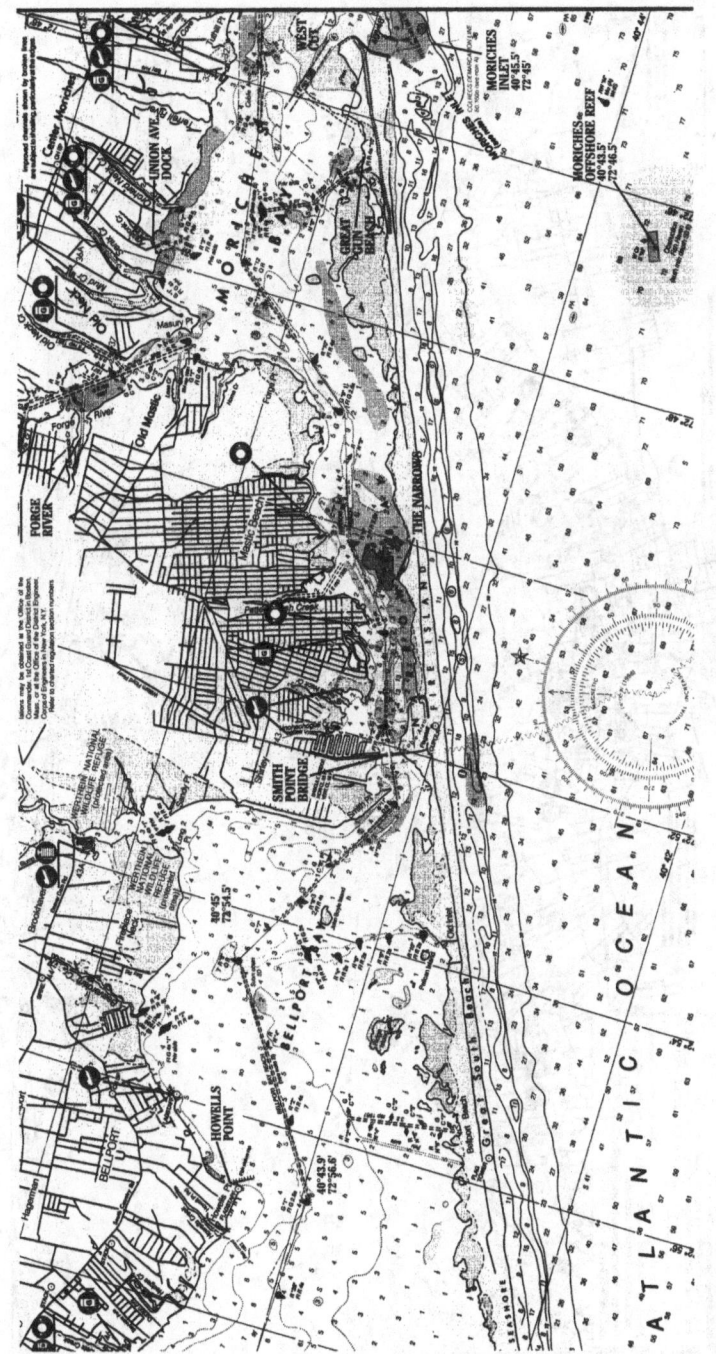

Fire Island 3

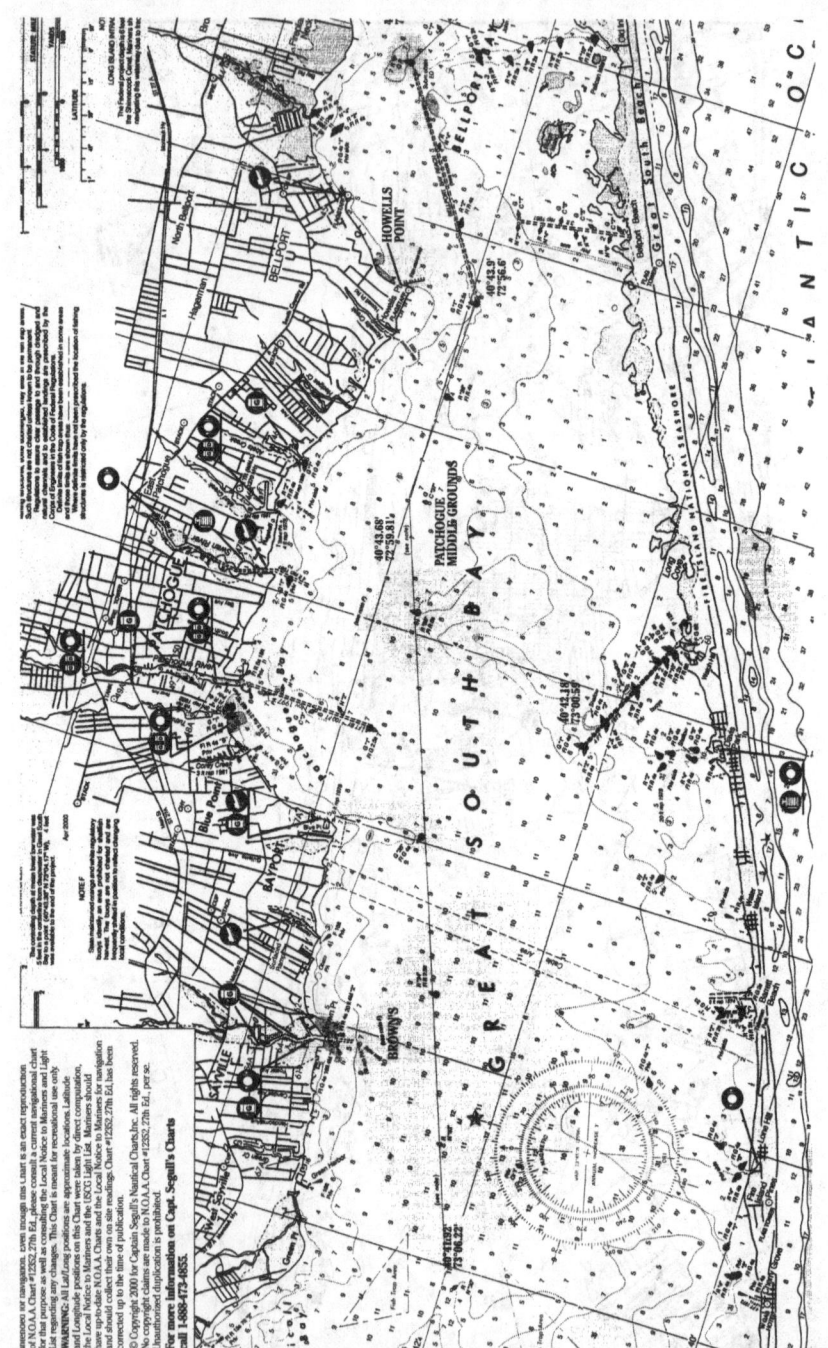

Fire Island 4

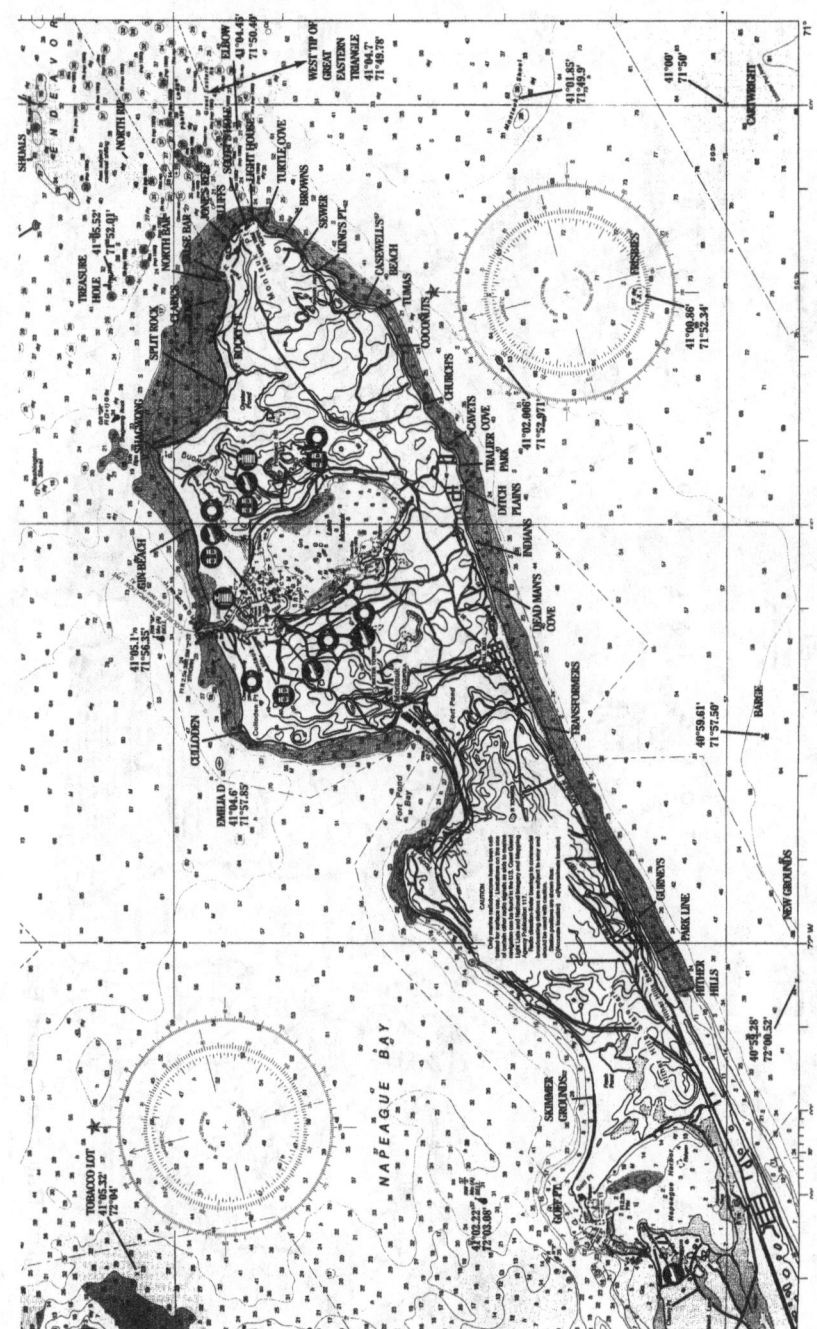

Montauk Point

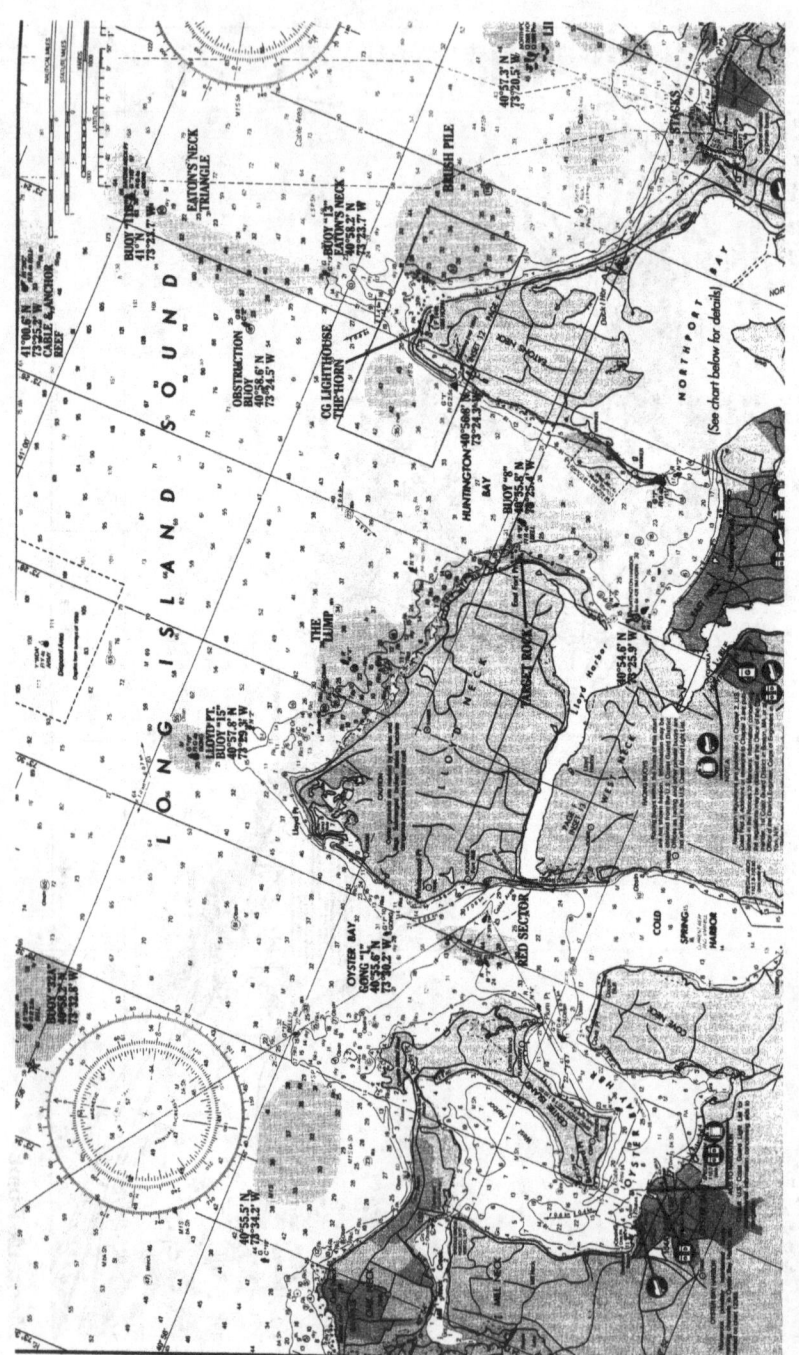

Huntington Bay and Oyster Bay

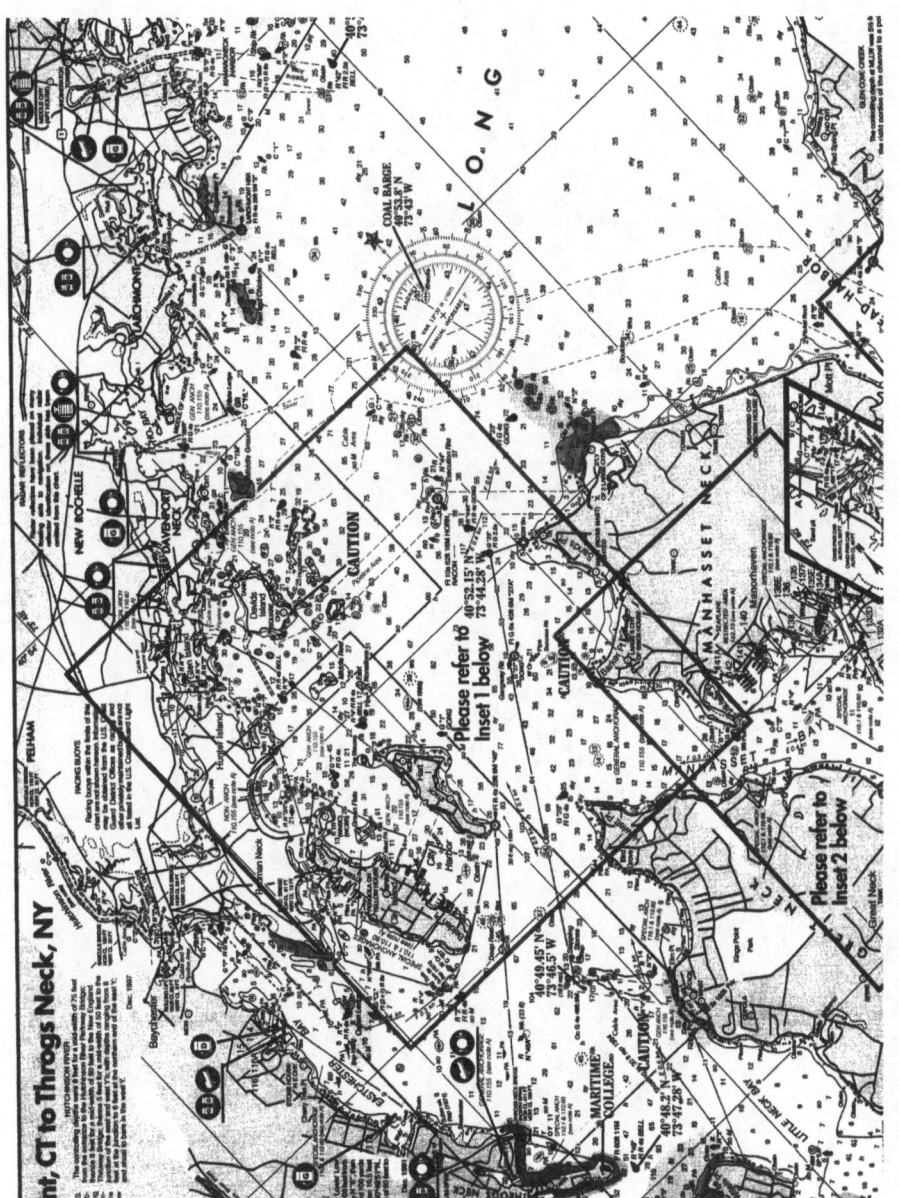

City Island to Execution Rock

www.ingramcontent.com/pod-product-compliance
Lightning Source LLC
Chambersburg PA
CBHW011420070526
44584CB00026BA/3782